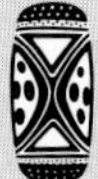

THE INSTITUTE REPORT SERIES

CONSERVING AUSTRALIAN ROCK ART

A MANUAL FOR SITE MANAGERS

DAVID LAMBERT

NSW National Parks and Wildlife Service, Gosford

EDITED BY GRAEME K. WARD

Australian Institute of Aboriginal Studies, Canberra

ABORIGINAL STUDIES PRESS • CANBERRA 1994

FIRST PUBLISHED IN 1989 BY

Aboriginal Studies Press
for the Australian Institute of Aboriginal Studies
GPO Box 553, Canberra, ACT 2601.

REPRINTED IN 1994 BY

Aboriginal Studies Press for the Australian Institute of Aboriginal and Torres Strait Islander Studies, GPO Box 553, Canberra, ACT 2601.

The views expressed in this publication are those of the author and not necessarily those of the Australian Institute of Aboriginal and Torres Strait Islander Studies.

NATIONAL LIBRARY OF AUSTRALIA CATALOGUING-IN-PUBLICATION DATA

Lambert, David 1949- .
Conserving Australian rock art.

Bibliography.
Includes index.
ISBN 0 85575 210 6.
ISSN 1030 6544.

1. Petroglyphs — Australia — Conservation and restoration — Handbooks, manuals, etc. 2. Rock paintings — Australia — Conservation and restoration — Handbooks, manuals etc. [3]. Aborigines, Australian — Art — Conservation and restoration — Handbooks, manuals etc. I. Ward, Graeme, 1943- . II. Australian Institute of Aboriginal Studies. III. Title. (Series: Institute report series).

709.01130994

DESIGNED BY Aboriginal Studies Press.
PRINTED IN AUSTRALIA BY Union Offset Co Pty Ltd, Canberra.

500 06 94

FRONT COVER Peter Sullivan carrying out conservation work at Nourlangie Gallery, Kakadu National Park. Photograph by Ivan Haskovec, Australian National Parks and Wildlife Service, Darwin, reproduced by courtesy of the Australian National Parks and Wildlife Service, Canberra.

CONTENTS

ILLUSTRATIONS

FIGURES

TABLES

PLATES

FOREWORD

by W. Dix

This manual for conservators and managers of rock art in Australia is a product of the Rock Art Protection Program, the second to be published in the Report Series of the Australian Institute of Aboriginal Studies. The Report Series was established as a relatively quick and inexpensive means of disseminating information to researchers and others working in the area of Aboriginal studies. The first volume of work funded by the Rock Art Protection Program to be published resulted from the research by Darryl Lewis and Deborah Rose in the Victoria River region: *The Shape of the Dreaming: The Cultural Significance of Victoria River Rock Art* (Aboriginal Studies Press 1988).

The Rock Art Protection Program was established by the Australian Institute of Aboriginal Studies in 1986 in response to a request from the then Minister for Aboriginal Affairs, the Hon. Clyde Holding. The Minister and his successor have provided extra funding to the Institute for this purpose and each year it has been possible to fund about twelve worthwhile projects which further the aims of conservation of this major aspect of Australia's heritage. Conservation projects have been carried out in all Australian states and the Northern Territory. Several sites have been fenced to protect them from stock; others have had protective barriers and walkways built to encourage visitors to keep their distance from rock faces exhibiting painted or engraved figures. In addition, informative signs have been erected at many sites and educational brochures provided for visitors.

Conserving Australian Rock Art: A Manual for Site Managers is the distillation of the author's many years of experience as a conservator and fieldworker. David Lambert has a wide understanding of his subject, and I am confident that this manual will be of considerable use to site managers and especially to the Aboriginal sites officers, rangers and others who are increasingly taking on responsibility for managing their own community's sites. I recommend it to all those interested in rock art and the problems of its conservation.

W. Dix
Principal
Australian Institute of Aboriginal Studies

FOREWORD by G. Ward

This manual is based on David Lambert's report of a project which was one of twelve supported under the Rock Art Protection Program from funds provided to the Australian Institute of Aboriginal Studies by the Minister for Aboriginal Affairs in the financial year ending 1987.

The initial stimulus for the study which formed the basis of this manual came from Sharon Sullivan, a member of the Council of the Australian Institute of Aboriginal Studies. Sharon Sullivan was convenor of the Institute's Rock Art Working Group and of the meeting later that year of the initial Rock Art Protection Program Executive Committee. The proposal for a conservation manual put forward by Lambert and considered at that meeting was funded along with eleven other projects (Ward and Sullivan have provided a description of the background to the development of this program).

David Lambert took six months' leave of absence from his position at the Gosford District office of the New South Wales National Parks and Wildlife Service to research the subject and to prepare the manual. That he was the appropriate person for the task was clear from his considerable involvement with conservation research. David graduated from Macquarie University in 1972 with geology as the major subject in his Bachelor's Degree. Since 1977 he has carried out conservation work on pictographs and petroglyphs for the New South Wales National Parks and Wildlife Service, and has also contributed his expertise to solving problems at sites elsewhere in Australia. From placing driplines and removing graffiti at Aboriginal sites in New South Wales and Queensland, he has moved to researching pigment loss, algae infestation and the development of visitor facilities in National Parks. Recently he produced a conservation strategy for historic engravings on Garden Island for the New South Wales National Parks and Wildlife Service.

As part of the current work, David visited sites all over Australia to familiarise himself with conservation problems peculiar to different regions and to take up the particular concerns of site managers. His broad understanding of the problems faced by conservators and his direct experience in working with a range of particular sites is evident in his discussion of the many topics covered in this report.

The manual has been designed for easy reference. There is a detailed summary under major and minor headings at the front and these headings are repeated in distinctive type throughout. A detailed index will facilitate its use. On one hand, the manual will be comprehensible to the site manager in the field who will be able to plan and undertake basic work at many types of sites; on the other, it will provide the fieldworker with sufficient understanding of the problems involved to know when to call in the expert conservator. It has been kept brief by eliminating much background or detailed explanatory material which might have duplicated that provided by Andrée Rosenfeld in her study (1985) of deterioration and conservation of prehistoric pictures in Australia. The two volumes might be used in conjunction.

A volume such as Lambert's *Conserving Australian Rock Art: A Manual for Site Managers* has long been sought by those interested in the research into and preservation of petroglyphs and pictographs in Australia; it is hoped that the publication of this book will assist site managers and fieldworkers and ultimately the aims of conservation. I wish to thank Ivan Haskovec, of the Australian National Parks and Wildlife Service, Darwin, for providing the photograph used for the cover.

Graeme Ward
Research Officer Sites
Australian Institute of Aboriginal Studies
June 1989

ACKNOWLEDGEMENTS

Producing this manual has involved fieldwork and the compilation of a report from information collected by the author and drawn from the work of other researchers. I structured the six month project in this way: I compiled a preliminary draft, drawing upon my own experience and various reports, in order to determine the overall content of the manual and to prompt feedback early in the project; I followed this first draft with fieldwork predominantly in areas of Australia with which I was unfamiliar (my field experience had been limited to New South Wales, the Australian Capital Territory and Central Queensland); this was necessary in order to give the manual a national perspective. As project time was fast running out, the second draft of the manual could be circulated only to a few people.

Many people and organisations greatly assisted the project. Firstly I would like to acknowledge the New South Wales National Parks and Wildlife Service for allowing and assisting me to undertake this study. I am most grateful to Sharon Sullivan for her continual support and for making detailed comment on the two drafts. Josephine Flood and Andrée Rosenfeld provided detailed comments and gave valued suggestions regarding the content of the manual.

For their comments on the first draft I would like to thank Graeme Ward and Kingsley Palmer (Australian Institute of Aboriginal Studies), Colin Pearson (Canberra College of Advanced Education), Don Hough (Victoria Archaeological Survey), John Clarke (Premier's Department, Perth), Grahame Walsh (Queensland National Parks and Wildlife Service), John Clegg (University of Sydney), George Chaloupka (Northern Territory Museum of Arts and Sciences), Mike Rowland (Heritage Unit, Department of Environment and Conservation, Brisbane), Peter Randolph (Western Australian Museum), Bronwyn Conyers (New South Wales National Parks and Wildlife Service), and Jane Jacobs (University of Adelaide).

During the fieldwork component of this study, many people and organisations provided valuable support and assistance. The Queensland National Parks and Wildlife Service provided transport to remote parts of Queensland, including Hook Island and the Flinders Island Group; assisting with fieldwork there were Dennis Devine and Chris Fowley, while Peter Hunnan and Grahame Walsh provided much of the organisational input for this work. At Lawn Hill National Park, Mic Almet and Colin O'Keefe assisted by directing me to sites. I thank all the staff at Conway National Park for their assistance during a busy period in their work schedule.

At Kakadu National Park, the hospitality and field assistance provided by Ivan Haskovec and Hilary Sullivan, together with support provided by the Australian National Parks and Wildlife Service generally, is gratefully acknowledged. In Victoria, Victoria Archaeological Survey staff directed me to sites; the services of Don Hough who accompanied me in the Black Range, the Grampians and Mount Pilot were very much appreciated.

The Aboriginal Heritage Branch of the South Australian Department of Environment and Planning provided much needed air transport into remote locations in the Mount Gammon and Flinders Ranges; in particular I thank Ross Muegge and Des Coulthard for their valued assistance.

This project was funded by the Australian Institute of Aboriginal Studies, to which I am most grateful. In particular, I thank Graeme Ward, who has consistently supported and managed the project, particularly in the later stages of manuscript preparation. The photographs used here were all taken by the author with the exception of Plates 29 and 30, which kindly were provided by Pam Bagatella, medical photographer of Westmead Hospital, Sydney.

INTRODUCTION

Painting and engraving of rock is a worldwide phenomenon, the oldest surviving form of human expression. It is broadly divided into two types: rock paintings and drawings, jointly referred to as pictographs; and rock engravings, often referred to as petroglyphs. Drawings are pictures inscribed or chalked onto rock surfaces using dry pigments. Paintings are made by applying wet pigments by stenciling, finger-painting or by using brushes such as those formed from chewed sticks or more intricate ones using feathers. The pigments used in painting are usually naturally occurring minerals which are generally weathering products and hence very stable, longlasting, colour-fast compounds. Pictographs which survive today have been executed in rock caves, rock shelters or cliff faces where the images are partly protected from direct rain and sun. Petroglyphs have been created on rock surfaces by a subtractive process; the rock may be pecked, hammered or abraded to form outlined or infilled figures.

Petroglyph and pictograph sites have been recorded all over the world and are famous prehistoric places in France, Italy, Africa, the USSR, India, North and South America, and China, among others. They reflect human occupation from early times to the present. The Australian continent contains one of the most diverse and culturally significant bodies of paintings and engravings to be found anywhere in the world.

There are tens of thousands of such sites in Australia; they are distributed across the continent and are grouped into particular regions, each characterisable in terms of the style and methods of execution of the images which it contains. Until the beginning of the twentieth century, painting and engraving was practised by traditional Aboriginal land owners throughout the country, but today its practice is restricted to a few areas. From the time that painting or engraving of a site finishes the action of natural processes leads to a deterioration of the condition of the images. The lack of repainting (or 'maintenance') of sites by traditional owners combined with this natural deterioration and the destruction of sites by human activities has produced a rapid decline in the amount of surviving imagery and its condition.

Many Australians consider that, because the images on rock have lasted so long already, their survival is secure and there is therefore no urgency for their conservation. But many such sites are not very ancient, and it is a fact that, where they are not being maintained, images have been and continue to be lost, both through weathering processes and human activities. Throughout Australia, pictures comprise a non-renewable resource which is in various stages of deterioration; it does need active conservation. It is the purpose of this manual to help site managers recognise the various sources of deterioration and threat and to know either how to deal with them, or when to call for expert assistance. In this way, the life of sites can be prolonged many times over.

This manual deals with the problems which cause the images to deteriorate. It outlines the techniques presently used by conservators to overcome those problems. These include: methods of treating and/or preventing direct water wash over pictographs; reduction or removal of damaging salts introduced by water seepage; lessening frost damage; and the effects of dust, soil, and plant cover. It also covers the treatment and prevention of animal and insect damage; methods for removing microflora such as algae, fungi and lichens; visitor management; and preventing and treating site vandalism. Methods of monitoring sites are also discussed.

The methods and techniques for conserving pictographs and petroglyphs in Australia have been developed and tested over a number of years. An important gathering of site managers and conservators was the 1977 International Workshop on the Conservation of Rock Art in Perth organised by the Institute for the Conservation of Cultural Material. It was apparent that while there were a number of dedicated workers in the field of recording and management of petroglyph and pictograph sites, there was only one full-time conservator. This was John Clarke, who was then employed by the Western Australian Museum and whose work formed the basis for many of the conservation practices adopted in this manual.

Under the National Estates Grants Program of 1983-84, Andrée Rosenfeld produced a technical report called *Rock Art Conservation in Australia*, which was later published by the Australian Heritage Commission (1985). This excellent book surveys the state of knowledge on deterioration processes and conservation and restoration measures. This manual is directed towards implementing those and other management and conservation strategies with a view to complementing the report. Accordingly, to avoid unnecessary duplication, frequent reference is made to Rosenfeld's work in this manual.

The need for a manual on the conservation of rock art was first identified by the Australian Institute of Aboriginal Studies following a meeting in 1980 called by the Joint Australian Academies (of Humanities and Sciences)

Committee for the Protection of Prehistoric Places. In 1986 the Minister for Aboriginal Affairs provided funds for the protection and preservation of Aboriginal rock art. The Australian Institute of Aboriginal Studies was charged with administering those funds, and established a Rock Art Working Group which later supported this six month project.

Good conservation practice dictates proper consultation and adherence to agreed standards and conventions. This manual assumes that readers are committed to these principles. In particular, the two following points are absolutely basic to good conservation practice in Australia and are assumed to be an integral part of all the procedures which follow.

In areas where traditional Aboriginal owners are present, permission must be sought for all conservation work undertaken. Similarly, in areas with Aboriginal representation, for example, where Land Councils are established, consultation is a necessary prerequisite to the conservation process. (See Sullivan 1985.)

The revised Burra Charter was adopted by Australia ICOMOS (International Council on Monuments and Sites) in 1981 and ratified by the Australian Government. Accordingly, any person undertaking work on sites is bound by the rules and principles contained therein. The Charter provides definitions and applies rules to be followed in conservation processes and practices. Adherence to these greatly reduces the risk of error in the application of conservation techniques. The Burra Charter is reprinted in Appendix 3.

This manual is intended to assist site managers who have received on-site training in conservation methods. By providing conservation information and pointing out the complexities of seemingly straightforward problems, the risk of damage to sites by well-intentioned personnel will be reduced. The aim of this manual is to make managers better equipped to recognise and to undertake straightforward conservation work while at the same time recognising more complex undertakings and, accordingly, seeking appropriate professional help.

1. THE IMPACT OF SURFACE WATER

Direct water erosion

While slow water seepage emanating from within the rock face sometimes results in a protective mineralised cover (Lambert 1980), a rapid water flow, especially from surface runoff, generally results in erosive action on pictograph surfaces. Prevention of erosive action of water in shelters is quite straightforward, requiring only simple water diversion techniques and driplines. One difficulty appears to be in assessing the problem, particularly in areas where driplines have not previously been placed. The results of direct water erosion are as follows:

1. There is often a sharp vertical-tending division of image and clean stone. This is most commonly distinguished by a white zone by the side of a black zone, of either mineral or organic composition (Plates 1 and 2 and Figure 1).
2. Figures are often cut vertically. This dividing line may be either sharp or gradual.

Direct water erosion is more commonly evident (a) in areas where rainfall is heavy but sporadic (eg, arid areas); (b) on boulders where the shelter profile is shallow and no definite natural dripline is present in the shelter.

Damage by water seepage is much less common and takes on a different form by emanating from line or point sources (Figure 2).

Mineral accretion

Accretions of minerals can obliterate painted surfaces. (The matter is dealt with fully by Rosenfeld 1985:21-25.) While the composition of the surface-forming minerals can sometimes be very complex, by far the most common is silica (also referred to as silcrete), particularly in sandstone shelters.

In the field, the silica will vary in appearance from a coating which is invisible to the naked eye (but detectable using scanning electron microscopy), to a thick milky-white coating which can obscure the image (Plates 3 and 4). Some silica formation is advantageous, however, and it appears to be the best known preserver of paintings. (See Chapter 7: Washing for further discussion of surface mineralisation.) An answer to long-term conservation of pictographs may well lie in this mechanism. The most likely source of silica is

Figure 1

Typical colour succession following water damage: Taken from Plate 1, this figure demonstrates the typical colour succession present at sites where surface water flow is evident. The water flow line is often marked by a white salt zone followed by a black salt zone (calcium oxalate), which grades into clean rock or painted surface.

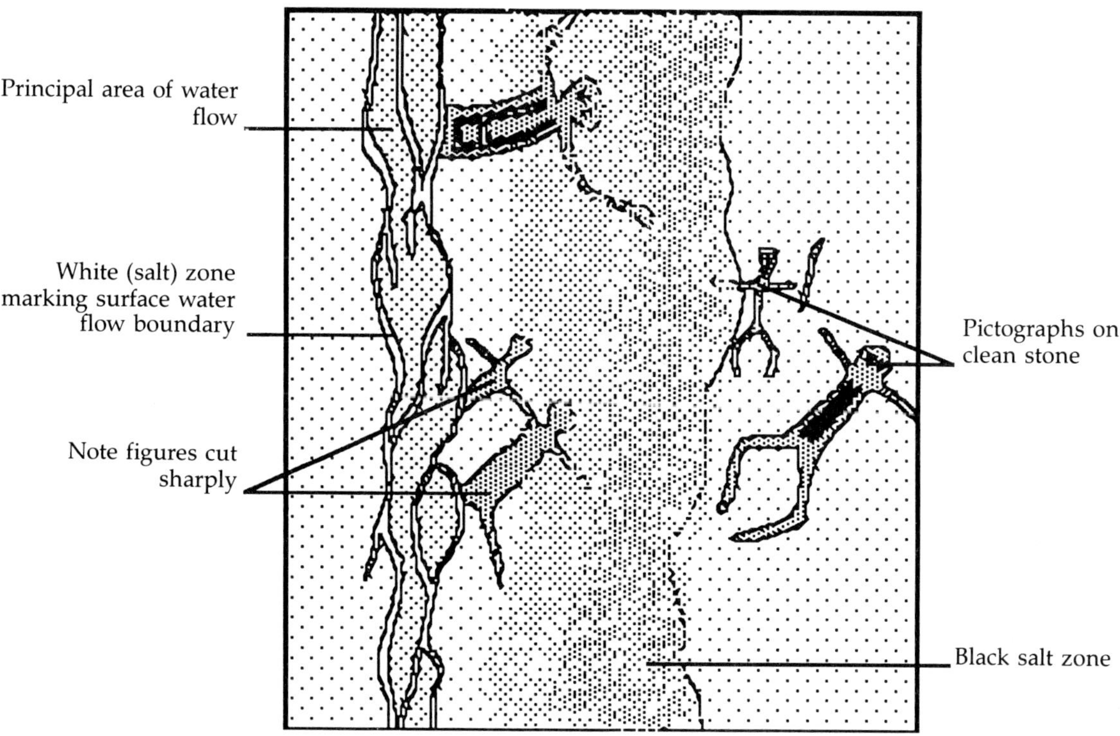

ground water which may be observed seeping through cracks and point sources in the shelter wall (Figure 3).

Frost damage

Frost weathering in the form of flaking or exfoliation of the rock surface is most likely to take place in the cold climate areas of Australia. The mechanism is quite simple; there is a spontaneous expansion of water from the liquid phase to the ice phase. In addition, following confined freezing, pressure increases by about 1750 p.s.i. for each degree Celsius of temperature decrease down to minus 22 degrees Celsius (Winkler 1973:177).

Whereas frost weathering is an area of major concern in colder countries like Canada (Wainwright 1985:25), there is no documentation of Australian sites. Observation at sites in colder climates of the Australian Capital Territory and the New England area of New South Wales would suggest that frost damage may play a role in site deterioration. Water and green algae have been found to be present behind rock flakes in granite boulder shelters in both of these locations, and it is difficult to believe that frost damage would not result. The type of damage considered to be caused by this process is shown in Plate 5.

An additional point worthy of consideration here is that the coldest parts of Australia—Tasmania, the Snowy Mountains, the New England Tablelands and the Victorian Alps—contain very few or no rock paintings. This may not mean that images were not painted in these areas but, rather, that many prehistoric pictographs have been lost through exfoliation due to frost shattering.

The treatment for water-related deterioration, other than salt damage, is the same in all cases. If the area to be protected can be kept continually dry then adverse impacts from direct water erosion, mineral accretion and frost will cease.

Water diversion outside the shelter should always be considered, but in practice is only applicable to a small number of sites. Surface drainage channels built on or upslope from the roof of the shelter may successfully divert water away from the site before it reaches the natural or artificial dripline.

Figure 2

Effects of water seepage: This diagram is adapted from a site near Inverell, New South Wales. It demonstrates a different type of surface water damage to that shown in Figure 1. In this case, motifs are being removed by water seepage through the rock rather than over the surface. Driplines are not appropriate, but rather the source of water needs to be found and diverted away from the site.

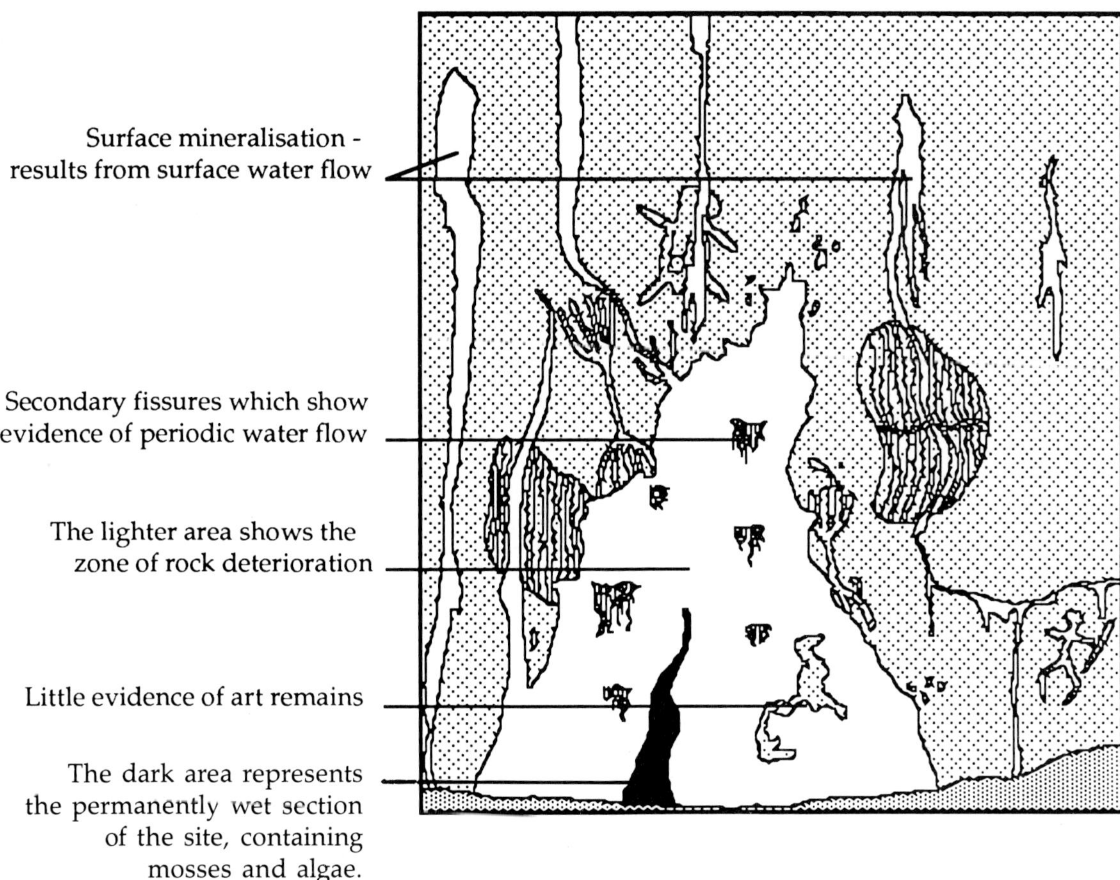

Driplines and silicone products

The aim of artificial dripline placement is to improve the efficiency of the natural dripline of a shelter. As water and silicone have very poor surface adhesion, water will fall freely upon hitting the silicone bead, which forms the artificial dripline. A frequent misconception is that the dripline channels water along its course. This of course is not true and has probably resulted from the use of the term 'water diversion'.

Effective placement of silicone driplines and silicone fillers is well documented. The procedures detailed below have been taken from Clarke (1979) and Gillespie (1983:194-97).

Applying silicone bead driplines

It is important to use a product which will tolerate ultraviolet radiation and other weathering agents. Two products which have proven to be satisfactory are 'Selleys 781' window glass (clear) sealant (available in 310g cartridges) and 'Ramset RB833' silicone rubber (clear).

Determine approximately where the dripline is to go on the rock surface (Figure 4). Once the ideal location is determined consider where the water will be directed. Will splash be a problem? What about the impact of water upon the floor deposit? Be prepared to make compromises and move the location of the dripline to suit. Just as important are aesthetic considerations. If possible the dripline should be placed at some distance from the imagery, preferably high up where it is less obvious and out of reach.

In order to obtain a satisfactory bond to the rock surface a clean substrate is essential. Scrub clean the track of the dripline using a wire brush and methylated spirits. Next, use a 5mm light bristle brush to apply a fine, light track of 'Ramset PR001' primer and allow it to dry for ten minutes. (If this primer is unavailable then commercial grade toluene or acetone is satisfactory.)

Apply the silicone using a standard gun or dispenser. It is important to apply steady pressure to the gun in order to obtain an even bead of silicone. The nozzle should be angled in towards the rock to obtain good rock surface contact (Plate 6). It has been shown by Gillespie (1983) that by cutting the nozzle to an inverted-V shape the cross-section of the dripline is sharpened and results in a more efficient dripline. A practice run of the whole procedure is very advisable.

Figure 3

Silica accretion process and detail of seepage zone: Silica mineralisation has been observed below water seeps coming from within the rock.

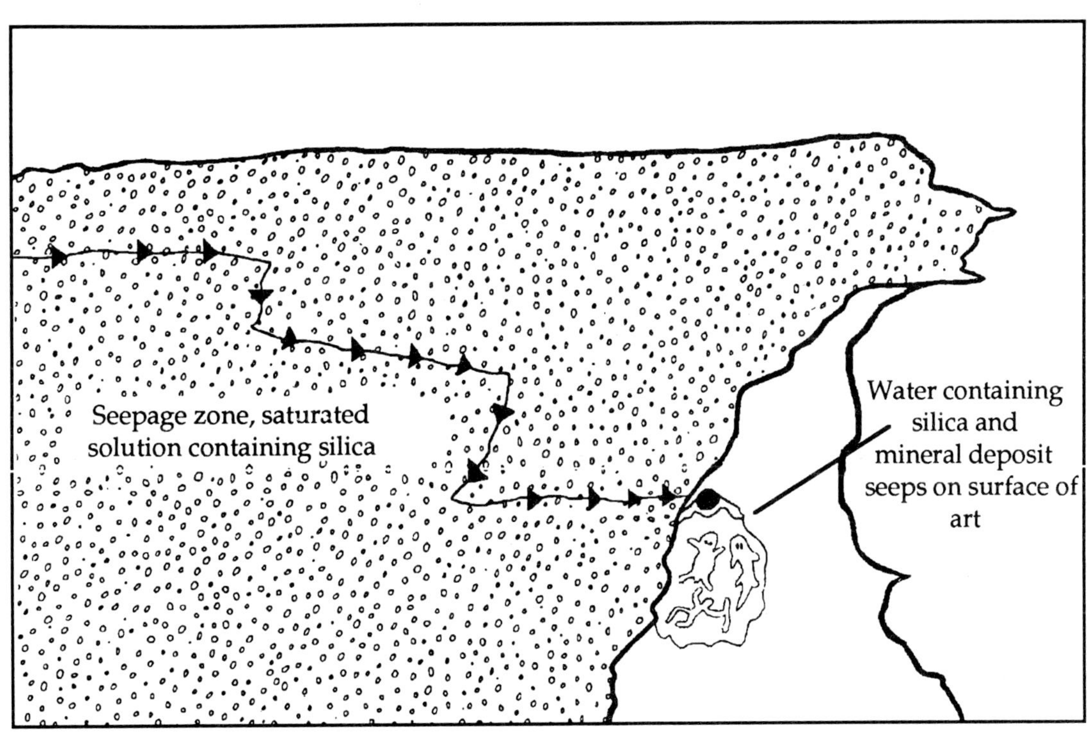

DETAIL OF SEEPAGE ZONE

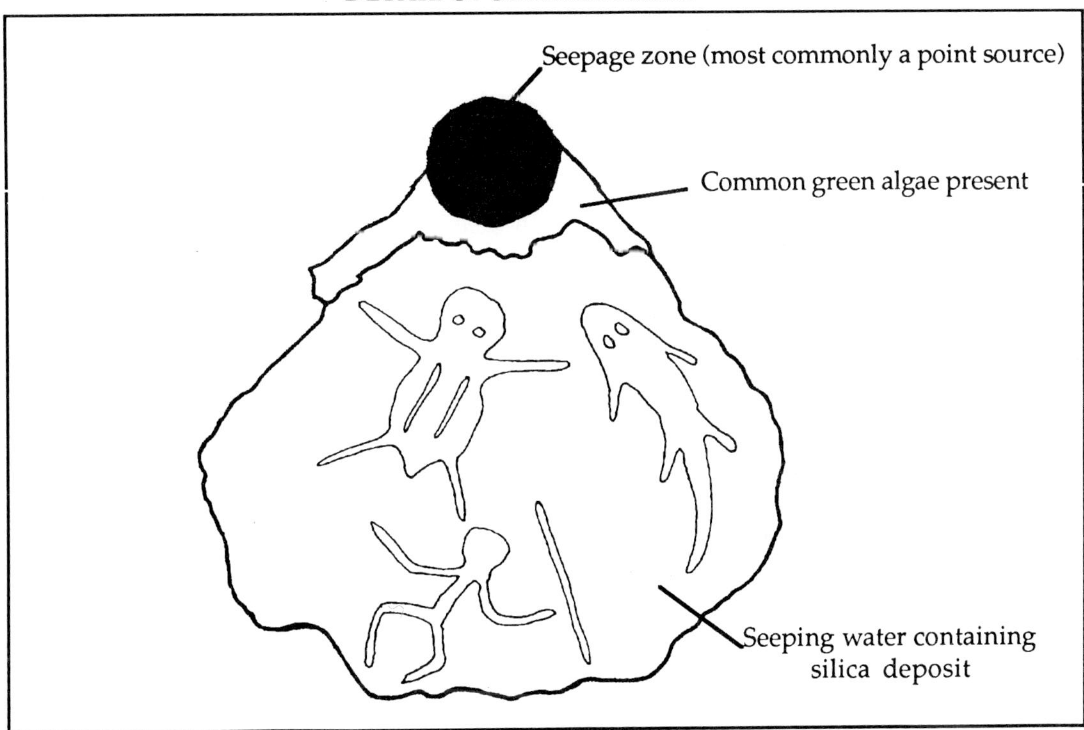

Monitoring driplines

As with all site management, a maximum but practical level of monitoring and maintenance is recommended. The dripline may be peeled off by inquisitive visitors, or a poor silicone to rock bond may have gone unnoticed. Positioning of the dripline may have been inadequate for the conditions experienced at the site. Any of these inadequacies will show up with time and, if the sites are revisited at later dates, these faults quickly can be remedied.

In addition, long-term and unforeseen problems may result from dripline placement. For example, a thick, black, soot-like material, first identified by North and Clarke (1987) as whewellite (calcium oxalate dihydrate) at Cannon Hill in Kakadu National Park, is observed in dry, concave sections in the roof of shelters. While the mechanism and time of formation of this surface-coating mineral is not clearly understood, it is a reasonable possibility that it may form in the dryer environment created by the use of driplines and that, if formation does occur, it may be several years before it is detected. In short, the long-term impact of driplines on sites is not known. This introduces a twofold obligation on the site conservator and the controlling authority:

1. They should observe repeatedly a sample of sites where driplines have been introduced for any adverse effects (at approximately two-yearly intervals).
2. They must be prepared to remove driplines if long-term adverse impacts result.

This procedure is in accordance with Article 2 of the Burra Charter (1981).

While the use of silicone driplines is a reversible technique, it is difficult and time consuming to remove completely the dripline when it has been correctly applied. Although the main bead of silicone may be quickly removed, usually a thin skin of silicone remains firmly attached to the rock and this may act effectively as a dripline. It can only be removed by painstaking wire-brushing. Accordingly, it is recommended that a conservative approach to dripline placement be taken by the relevant authorities; driplines should only be applied in situations where actual or likely figure-cutting by surface water can be demonstrated (Plate 1). In shelters where images are believed to be very old (for example, the pre-estuarine painting in Kakadu National Park), it is considered that driplines are only warranted when evidence is present of changed environmental circumstances which present a short-term threat to the survival of the images.

Figure 4
Artificially changing direction of surface water flow in a dripline: Shelter profile showing changed direction of surface water flow following application of a dripline.

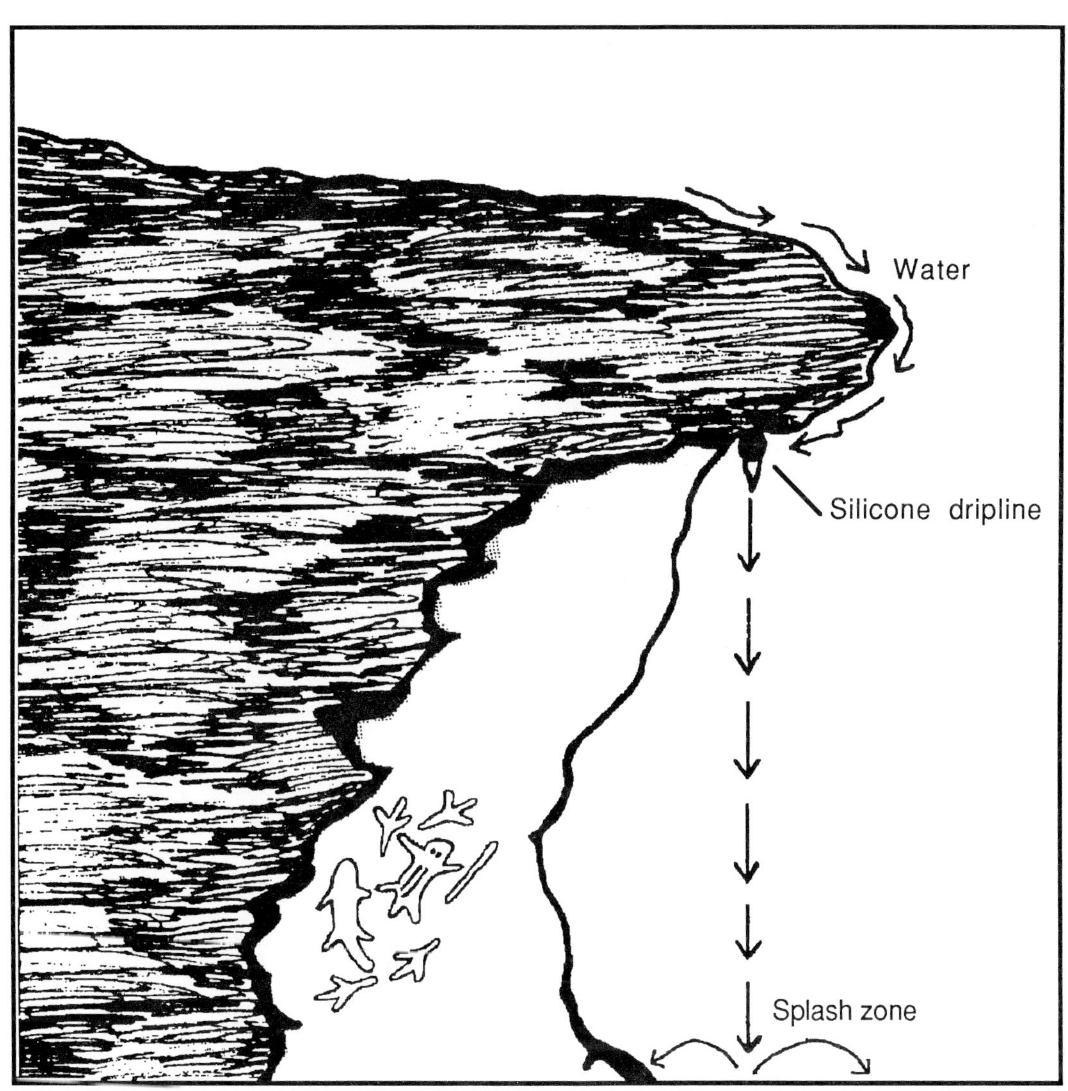

Driplines using silicone water repellant

An effective and visibly less obvious dripline can be produced by applying silicone water repellant to the drip area (J Clarke, personal communication, 1987). Coating a band of rock approximately 200mm wide usually is sufficient, although this can be made as wide as necessary to divert the amount of surface water present at a particular site.

Application of the water repellant may need to be repeated every five years to rejuvenate the treated area. The great advantage of this newer and somewhat less proven technique is that the material used cannot be seen, although in some cases a colour contrast may be present where it is necessary to clean the rock surface before applying the band of water repellant.

The products recommended for use include 'Raffles' and 'Vessey' silicone water repellants. These are applied most conveniently and accurately using an airless spray gun. Silicone water repellant may also be applied by brush but run-marks and splash are difficult to avoid. Again it is advisable to treat a trial area first and test the efficiency of the dripline thus formed by spraying water above it. It is best to carry out the trial a small distance away from the main area to be treated as the rock surface must be completely dry before applying the repellant.

Redirecting water emanating from cracks or fissures

This problem is mainly confined to Kakadu (Gillespie 1983:197, 205) but may apply elsewhere. The surface preparation procedure is similar to that used for the installation of silicone driplines. When dry, narrow cracks or fissures may be filled directly with silicone building sealant. However, when the cracks are large (ie, greater than about 4mm), a product known as 'Schlarge' foam (also known by ICI as 'backer rod' or more fully as 'closed-cell polyethylene backer rod') is used to fill the spaces before applying the silicone sealant. 'Schlarge' foam comes in the form of compressible foam rods of various diameters and can be easily compressed to fill an uneven crack or void. The seeping water must then be diverted to a safe area of discharge. (See also Chapter 2: Water diversion.)

2. SALT DETERIORATION

Salt decay

In recent times the mechanism of stone decay has been well documented by Winkler (1973), Lambert (1980), Lewin (1982) and Amoroso and Fassina (1983). The process of salt decay is discussed by Rosenfeld (1985:34-36). The phenomenon applies particularly to Australia (Wainwright 1985:25) and occurs most commonly in sandstone rocks. In simple terms surface sandstone containing approximately one per cent by weight of salt will be soft and badly deteriorated. Salt weathering of sandstone is most evident in shelters and takes the appearance of fresh white stone, usually on a vertical face with a deposit of clean white sand at its base. The erosion zone often takes a scallop-shaped form which may range from several centimetres to several metres across.

The salt is most likely to be derived both from rainwater, which contains low concentrations of salt, and ground water which will give a more local flavour to the final salt composition. The salt is concentrated and builds up in areas of evaporation in shelters which are not being flushed by rainwater (Figure 5).

The rate of erosion of sandstone in a section of shelter with salt decay is extremely high and of the order of 0.1mm per year (Lambert 1980:32). This mechanism is thus a major factor in the weathering of sandstone shelters (Plate 7). It is interesting to note from this study that salt decay is also prevalent in inland shelters and is by no means restricted to seaspray situations.

Salt damage has also been observed in pigments at Delemere (Plate 8) and in Kakadu in the Northern Territory. Treatment of this type of damage requires specialist skills and should not be attempted by site managers.

A special case of salt weathering is provided by Walsh (1984:126). His discussion was occasioned by the observation of the almost total absence of imagery in the numerous rock shelters of such areas as the Murphy Range of the Central Highlands of Queensland, known to have concentrated Aboriginal habitation. Closer examination shows that the often sweeping and scalloped overhangs of the Hutton Sandstone which comprises this range tend to weather in a manner different from most other locations. It is one of the major water-bearing sandstones, and tends to weather evenly all over its cavern surfaces, effectively shedding its entire surface area at an unknown, but

Figure 5
Salt weathering: Rock cross-section demonstrating salt weathering process in shelters.

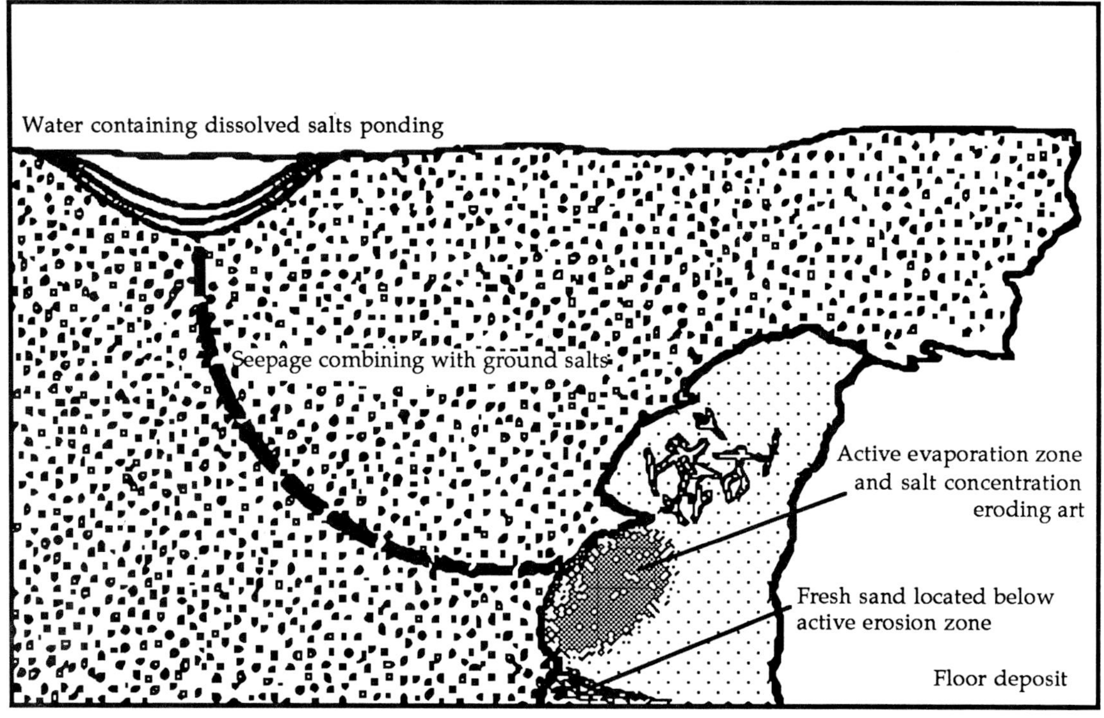

apparently fairly rapid rate. This varies from the more common sectional weathering traits of most other local sandstones, and probably accounts for the almost entire absence of any evidence of images in the Murphy Range shelters. In less extreme cases where images remain to be conserved, a sand sample of deteriorated stone may be sent for chemical analysis to confirm this deterioration process.

The impact of erosion by salt action at open sites such as sandstone engravings (petroglyphs) is unknown. Engravings (even post-contact figures) observed near the ocean generally show considerable wear with groove relief often being faint. This, combined with other factors such as rock colour, suggests that salt erosion may well take place in a different form to that shown in shelters where the salt decay rate is certainly greater.

Treatment of salt decay

Treatment for salt rock weathering has had mixed success. The practice in building conservation is to separate the deteriorating stone from the water source by putting some form of damp course in place. Thus by removing the cause, any further damage is prevented. With rock shelters, the use of a damp course is impractical and other less effective but often very helpful steps may be taken.

Water diversion

With regard to water diversion outside the shelter, it is sound conservation practice to keep sites as dry as possible. Check that water does not collect on the roof of the shelter where it is slowly directed towards the painted surfaces through porous rock or through cracks and fissures in the roof. At Mount Grenfell, near Cobar in western New South Wales, water was diverted from the roof by removing soil and vegetation from the roof and allowing the water to run off by opening natural drainage lines to the side of the shelter. In addition, some minor drainage channels were built on the roof of the shelter using sand, cement and rock. In this way, runoff was directed away from the site.

At a granite boulder site near Inverell in New South Wales, it is planned to build a small roof over a tunnel-shaped feature that collects water which slowly seeps through cracks and fissures to the images. In this case the water collects only from direct rain and not from runoff.

Water flushing

Treatment of salt weathering by water flushing consists of spraying the affected area with fresh water to flush out soluble salts. Areas containing paintings or drawings should not be sprayed. This is simply a holding operation and has been observed to work in several Sydney sandstone sites. It is a treatment which can be employed where salt threatens to erode nearby images. In Sydney sandstone areas the method used is to spray water from a knapsack lightly onto the affected area at the rate of approximately twenty litres of water per square metre of salt-damaged rock.

There are some problems with this method, however. The spraying must be regularly repeated—in Sydney sandstone, approximately every one to two years. The resultant water runoff must be able to escape freely from the shelter without causing damage to other parts of the site or accumulating in the floor deposits.

It must be remembered that this method only helps to remove some of the accumulated salt, and that the source of the problem remains.

'Sacrificial render'

This method has not been used in the conservation of pictographs and petroglyphs but may well be employed as an improvement to the other treatments in an appropriate situation.

In some sandstone buildings salt attack has been treated by covering the damaged area with a lime and sand mortar mix (in the proportion of one to three) known as a 'render'. This render is porous, and moisture from the rock is drawn into it, resulting in the salts being deposited in the render rather than the rock. The render will slowly deteriorate and eventually have to be replaced but the rock will be protected from further attack.

Long-fibre tissue

Soluble salts located over and in painted surfaces can be removed by a series of distilled water poultices applied through a protective layer of long-fibre tissue paper (Schwartzbaum 1985:69). The poultices are allowed to dry and the process repeated until no salt efflorescence can be observed at the surface. This treatment can be applied where salts occur over paintings or drawings. While it is likely that most forms of long-fibre tissue would be suitable, I have personally used only one type, hemp paper, which I have found to be most satisfactory. This was obtained from a company in Japan (See Appendix 1);

however, it may prove more economical if an Australian supplier could be found.

Long-fibre tissue (also known as 'Japanese paper' or 'hemp paper'), is a long-fibre paper which maintains its strength when wet. It is used when working with water over water-sensitive pigment such as white clay, or in cases where pigments are loosely bonded to the rock surface. A small trial area should always be selected in an obscure part of the site before applying the technique over a large area. The method is as follows:

1. Lay or hold a dry sheet of the paper over the trial area. (The trial area should be positioned low down in the shelter to avoid water washing down onto figures below.)
2. Ease the water into the paper using a 200mm bristle brush. (The paper will cling to the surface when wet and will no longer need to be held in place.)
3. For poulticing, add several additional layers of paper by repeating this process.

Enclosing engravings

The construction of a roof over engravings has not been attempted in Australia, although there is currently a proposal to do so at a European engraving site at Garden Island in Sydney. At Provincial Park, Canada, an engraving site has been incorporated into a building for conservation and public display. This method of conservation may well be further developed in Australia as it simulates conditions present in shelters where the best preserved engravings have been observed.

3. SOIL AND VEGETATION

The impact of soil cover

Many engraving sites are being encroached by vegetation and the associated increased soil cover. In some cases the construction of walkways and increased visitation has led to increasing soil cover, mainly working in from the edges of engraved rock surfaces. In undisturbed, isolated sites it is frequently necessary to remove encroaching mosses and associated soil cover to reveal completely the engraved figures or petroglyphs.

By allowing rock to become soil covered we are effectively moving from a situation of predominantly mechanical weathering to one of chemical and microbiological weathering. Traditional weathering theory deals with both weathering types but does not compare the two in terms of weathering rates. Ollier (1976:248) commented that 'Chemical methods of determining weathering rates have rarely been applied to rocks other than limestone because of many complications'. Further, as Winkler (1975:161) notes:

> Microbiological attack is mostly chemical, by chemical secretion and photosynthetic activity, producing and accelerating chemical reactions and secreting organic acids which readily attack silicate minerals, carbonates and sometimes pyrite. Weathered rock surfaces may be populated by as many as one million bacteria per gram of rock, hundreds of thousands of fungi ...

Chemical weathering may render the rock more friable while at the same time leaving it structurally intact in appearance. For example, a five-point scale based on friability describes the most weathered example as '... soft rock that disintegrates when immersed in water' (Ollier 1976:127). Thus a freshly exposed engraving previously covered by moss or soil may appear sharp and intact (this may also be accentuated by the light colour of the exposed rock), but in truth it may be more friable and quickly lose any groove integrity once exposed. For example, at an engraving site at Bulgandry, near Gosford, New South Wales, the groove profile of over half of a figure from which soil was removed is considerably more weathered compared with the other half of the figure which was continuously exposed.

At Mount Cameron West in Tasmania, Hughes and others (1981) formulated a conservation strategy of continued sand cover for an engraving site executed on aeolian calcarenite which has been buried under sand for an estimated period of some 850 years. (Aeolian calcarenite is the weathered, re-cemented limestone existing along the northwestern shore of Tasmania.) During this time the rock had become extremely soft and friable and therefore very susceptible to mechanical weathering once exposed. Hughes quoted a study by Luckman (1951:6) in which it was noted that 'Where the covering sand was damp, particularly on horizontal surfaces, erosion was so advanced that the carved rock had literally merged into the sand itself ...'. The conservation strategy recommended for the site was to maintain a state of sand cover, as the engraved rock, although very friable, was stable under these circumstances.

A second case was noted by Wainwright (1985:28). In British Columbia severe exfoliation, compounded by vandalism, resulted in the authorities there burying an engraving site under 150mm of sand, topped with one metre of earth seeded with grain. Prior to burial the petroglyphs were accurately recorded by contour maps, drawings, photographs and latex moulding.

Theory and practice in this field apparently is inconsistent; is the covering of an engraving with soil, mosses or plants helpful or otherwise? From the evidence available the following general conclusions are drawn:

1. Soil cover will result in chemical weathering which in turn results in the rock fabric becoming friable. Mechanical weathering is, however, generally reduced.
2. The worst scenario is therefore one of repeated cover followed by exposure.
3. Accordingly, previously uncovered engravings should be kept clear of encroaching soil and vegetation.
4. Engravings which have been covered for long periods, resulting in a soft and friable rock fabric, should be left covered or, if exposed, consolidated in some way.

An example of the impact of soil cover on pictographs given by Walsh (1984:73) concerns the Cathedral Cave site in Carnarvon Gorge, Queensland. Here engravings extend down the main rock face for 900mm below the surface of the present earth floor. No ochre paintings have been observed below ground level yet they appear in abundance on the walls above. Walsh concluded that, in this case, the weathering below soil is significantly greater for pictographs, and pointed to other possible examples.

Flood (personal communication, 1987) advised of several examples in various parts of Australia where the lower part of figures painted on the wall of a rock shelter have disappeared, probably as the result of earth or occupation deposit building up and covering them. Indeed, this effect is often present above the floor level where the influence of dust or salt cover has removed or damaged pigments.

It would appear that earth and dust have a detrimental impact on pictographs and conservation efforts should be directed towards removal of soil cover and prevention of further build-up.

The impact of vegetation

Vegetation growing near sites may have both positive and negative implications for conservation. Positive impacts relate mainly to soil stabilisation which may help reduce the amount of free dust and soil that may become windblown or kicked up by visitors, particularly in an arid environment. Negative impacts may include physical damage by splitting of rock by tree roots, direct rubbing of plants on pigments, and damage by fire. Drastic changes to vegetation structure may also lead to alteration of microclimate, which in turn may result in the growth of moss and algae.

In the case of shelters, the splitting of rock by tree roots is documented by Walsh (1984:112-14) in the Central Highlands of Queensland, where the roots of Rock Fig trees penetrate narrow crevices, often leading to rock failure. In addition, fine primary roots have been observed spreading and bonding to painted rock surfaces, particularly in the moister monsoon climates of northern Australia. At Whale Cave, south of Sydney, New South Wales, cave roof failure, following mining subsidence, was observed partly to follow cracks caused by the roots of a eucalypt growing on the roof of the shelter.

Shrubs and trees have been observed growing close to or over painted rock surfaces. These have been reported in Kakadu by Chaloupka, Hughes, Watchman and Gillespie (1983:198). Large ferns were removed from Hands on the Rock Shelter in the Blue Mountains National Park in New South Wales. These ferns (specifically *Todeabarbara*) were rubbing directly on the rock surface, having already removed any pictographs at their attained height. Plants have been removed from sites at Lawn Hill National Park in North Queensland for similar reasons. In such cases the environmental factors of removal, together with the possibility that the removal of vegetation may give offence to Aboriginal custodians, must be taken into account. These considerations are weighed against existing and potential damage to the site if the vegetation is to remain, in terms of the risk of both physical damage and fire damage (Plate 9).

In a recent study, Haydock and Rodda (1986) manipulated the vegetation structure outside a large open shelter known as Walga Rock in Western Australia. Based on the weather model they had established for the site, they developed a suitable regime in order to protect the site from driving rain and at the same time, modify surface rock temperature fluctuation and maintain adequate ventilation to the site.

A final impact is considered here. Several cases are known where vegetation change has affected microclimate which has, in turn, resulted in the proliferation of microflora such as algae, fungi and moss. This phenomenon is dealt with in the next chapter.

Removal of soil cover

In the case of soil removal, the most difficult part is to decide whether the site warrants treatment. The washing method discussed here is similar to that described by Clarke (1978:93-94); modifications will need to be made according to the scale of the operation. Assessment by an archaeologist is necessary to check whether the site has sub-surface cultural deposits. The procedure recommended is as follows:

1. Determine the area to be cleaned. It may not be advisable to clear all soil and vegetation from the area. Pockets of vegetation, even if centrally located, may add to both the integrity and aesthetics of the site.
2. Remove vegetation with shovels or by hand, taking care not to scratch the rock surface.
3. Wash down the site, using anything from a knapsack spray to a water tanker or fire truck, depending on the scale of the operation. In order to avoid the risk of surface damage, no water jet should be used.
4. Treat small areas at a time and work down the slope. Some shoveling may be required to move accumulated soil.

For a small-scale operation (sites less than twenty square metres in area), it may be more practical to remove soil by dry-brushing and let future rain do the final washing down. The procedure recommended is as follows:

1. As in (1) above.

2. Carefully pull or peel back the vegetation by hand so as not to damage the imagery. If removed by hand, the vegetation will often take most of the soil with it.

3. If necessary, remove soil up to one metre from the edge of the site to avoid future build-up.

4. Remove excess soil with a shovel, provided this can be done without scratching the rock surface.

5. Allow time for the site to dry, if the remaining area is damp. The area may then be dry-brushed using 100mm bristle brushes or larger, soft nylon brushes, held in the hand.

6. Give some thought to providing simple drainage for the site and appropriate water diversion to avoid a repetition of the soil build-up process.

On a smaller-scale site, dry-brushing has several advantages over washing in that it can be applied in more isolated areas, and by hand-brushing, the operator can observe more closely the impact of the work on the site. Dry-brushing using soft bristle or nylon brushes will usually have minimal impact on rock surfaces.

Removal of vegetation

Preliminary considerations

Removal of vegetation is relatively straightforward, but these factors should be considered before proceeding:

1. Only undertake removal of vegetation where the damage or potential damage to the site is obvious (eg, direct rubbing, fire damage, etc).

2. Assess the consequences of vegetation removal. For example, allowing considerably more light into the shelter may result in adverse effects such as algal growth or the microclimate of the shelter may be altered, by permitting greater evaporation or increasing the likelihood of rain driving onto the rock.

3. Consider the aesthetics and integrity of the site.

4. Could removal of vegetation give offence to Aboriginal custodians? Consult them.

5. Identify the vegetation to be removed and determine if it is common to the area. If the plants are uncommon to the area, or food plants, they may have been planted by Aborigines and hence be part of the site (as was the case at Kenniff Cave, Central Queensland). It is possible that rare vegetation should not be removed; in such cases botanists should be consulted.

Guidelines

Upon proceeding, the following guidelines are suggested:

TREES: In cases of rock face splitting and root damage, the only solution is to cut down the tree and immediately paint the cut stump with neat 'Roundup' or another low-toxicity, low-volume, tree killer chemical.

BRANCH RUBBING: It is generally sufficient to cut only the offending branch.

OTHER VEGETATION: Where they present obvious fire damage risk and the site displays evidence of past fire damage such as exfoliation, or where direct rubbing occurs, taller shrubs should be removed. Two methods suggested are hand pulling or cutting. For re-sprouters, cut stumps should be painted with neat 'Roundup'.

SPINIFEX REMOVAL: Spinifex is a tall grass which may grow in arid or harsh environments. When fired it burns with intense heat which may result in exfoliation of large flakes of nearby rock. Substantial damage has been observed where spinifex grows near engraving sites. It is therefore necessary to keep these areas clear. This may be achieved in two ways: (a) remove clumps by hand or, if feasible, by bulldozer; (b) burn and reburn regrowth as soon as it will support a fire, preferably more frequently than every five years. This will result in a relatively cool fire which is unlikely to cause further damage to the sites.

The maximum heat generated from a spinifex fire will be attained after approximately twenty years growth (R Bradstock, personal communication, 1988). Also, most spinifex species regenerate by reseeding after fire. Care should be taken not to burn too large an area away from the site as the larger spinifex clumps provide habitats for reptiles and burrowing mammals.

4. MICROFLORA

Problems caused by microflora (algae, lichen, fungi, bacteria)

Microflora in the form of algae, fungi and lichens have been widely noted on paintings in shelters. Where microflora grow over images, they demonstrably obscure and hide pigments. In addition, they may act as a catalyst for other weathering processes by retaining water and disintegrating the substrate (Wainwright 1985). Several case studies are dealt with below.

A site in the Australian Capital Territory known as Nursery Swamp 2 is a granite shelter containing six ochre figures (Rosenfeld and Winston-Gregson 1983). A green algae or fungi was first observed in 1985 by archaeologists who had previously excavated the deposit in 1981, when the microflora had been notably absent. When I visited the site in 1986, the microflora were much in evidence and visibly obscuring the imagery. The only factors which go towards explaining such a dramatic change at the site were a combination of a severe bushfire, which may have allowed more light to enter the shelter by removing dense vegetation nearby, and a wet season which may have provided the necessary moisture.

A second example of proliferating microflora occurred at the Quiera site in Morton National Park in New South Wales (Plates 10 and 11). A black and white photo taken by Jack Cole around 1950 shows about half of the painted area of the shelter (Bindon 1976). Judging from this photo, around forty to fifty per cent of the pigment has flaked off or been obscured since the 1950s (K Officer, personal communication, 1987). Clearly the microflora have been a feature at this shelter for a considerable time and, indeed, some of the paintings in white pigment are on lichen-covered rock. Recently changed conditions, which have opened up the understorey vegetation to allow more light and possibly moisture to the site, indisputably have led to a dramatic resurgence of microbiological growth in these southern latitude sites.

To compound the problem further, quite the reverse situation applied in Central Queensland. Walsh (1984:113) noted that, in Queensland:

> A further conservation problem results from the trait of certain shrubs and small trees preferring to grow in quite dense stands close to site entrances and sandstone faces. Soapbush, quinine and black wattle are some of the chief offending species ... . At times their vegetation combines with such density that it creates a dark, moist atmosphere in the sheltered overhang. This is conducive to a surface moisture content increase in the

sandstone surface, a detrimental feature which accelerates deterioration and encourages regrowth of destructive moss and algae.

Thus the implication is that in the higher latitude, colder climate, removal of vegetation growing close to the site may lead to algal and fungal growth, whereas in the lower latitude, hotter climate, the reverse applies. It is not clear whether this is a function of altered light or moisture conditions at the site.

Lichen damage at a Sydney petroglyph site known as Devil's Rock at Burragurra, northwest of Gosford, New South Wales (Plate 12) has also been demonstrated (Lambert 1979). Trial techniques using fungicides such as 'Pentachlorophenol' to kill the microflora, combined with silicone water repellant to hinder recolonisation have resulted in retaining a clean, microflora-free sandstone surface for up to two years. However, a practice requiring repeated use of these chemicals would probably result in unacceptable environmental impact.

Removal of microflora

Article 23 of the Burra Charter would suggest that the first step in dealing with this problem is to identify the micro-organic material before proceeding with its removal. In practice, however, identification has proved extremely difficult and, with the limited resources available, simple removal of this material is strongly recommended where its damaging effects appear obvious.

This was the case of Nursery Swamp 2, where green algae was successfully removed in 1986. On a small trial area away from the paintings, the algae was easily removed by dry-brushing using a 75mm bristle brush. As the ochre figures were firmly bonded to the rock it was possible to extend this treatment over the painted surface with no observable detrimental impact on the pictographs.

The site known as Quiera, in southeastern New South Wales, had a much longer-standing yellow-green micro-organic growth (Plates 10 and 11). Around forty to fifty per cent of the clay pigment had been obscured since the site had been recorded in the late fifties. Microflora removal was not as straightforward as at the Nursery Swamp site. It was necessary to loosen the growth from the rock using bronze brushes, then 100mm bristle brushes. Because of the poor condition of the pigment and the weak pigment-to-rock bond, only very light brushing could be tolerated. Indeed, in some areas of the shelter it was only possible to remove microflora adjacent to figures, leaving the loosely bonded pigment with some microflora still attached. The last step was to wash both ends of the shelter where no paintings were present, to obtain more complete microflora removal in these areas.

Several points from these examples may be useful for fieldworkers.

1. Dry-brushing with soft brushes (bristle or bronze) is the most effective method of removing microflora with the least adverse effects.
2. Always test on a trial area in an obscure section of the shelter.
3. It is advisable to use a protective face mask containing dust collecting cartridges, particularly where large areas are to be cleaned.
4. It is desirable to conduct the work during a period of dry weather, as organic materials have the capacity to hold water and attempts to remove them in wet weather may result in smearing, making the job much more difficult.
5. The site will need monitoring to observe any recolonisation. If this occurs in any substantial way, chemical treatment of the site may be warranted after the repetition of the above steps, although in my experience, this has never been necessary. (See section below for details.)

The classic Australian experimental treatment of lichen was carried out by John Clarke in 1976 at Bolgart, Western Australia. His treatment of several open air engraving sites to remove lichen from granite rock tested the following agents:

TEST SITE 1: 'Lissapol N' detergent in water was used to wash the rock surface with scrubbing brushes. This is a non-ionic detergent which acts as a neutral wetting agent and is, to all intents and purposes, not considered an active chemical.

TEST SITE 2: These fungicides were applied: 'Pentachlorophenol', 'Panacide' (a BDH product), and 'Shirlon Plus' (ICI registered trade mark).

TEST SITE 3: Ammonium hydroxide (NH_40H) was used.

TEST SITE 4: Zinc fluorosilicate ($ZnSiF_6$) was used.

Following an inspection ten years after this experiment, Haydock and Rodda (1986:19) reported that all four treated granite surfaces were lichen-free. This experiment highlights the efficiency of removing microflora by non-chemical means. Simply washing the site, using the first method above, was sufficient in this case, without the potential complications added by the use of the toxic chemicals in methods 2, 3 and 4.

Organic material has been easily removed from Sydney engraving sites by a wet-brushing technique (see Chapter 7: Highlighting). The organic material in this case will, however, recolonise after approximately six to twelve months. An experiment by Clarke in 1977 (personal communication, 1978) on Sydney sandstone in which he used 'Pentachlorophenol' followed by treatment with silicone water repellant was somewhat longer lasting, it being approximately nineteen months before recolonisation occurred. Thus, in the more humid climate of the Sydney engravings we presently have no simple solutions for this problem.

5. ANIMALS

The impact of animals (insects, birds, macropods, stock)

Mud-building organisms cause widespread damage by constructing mud nests and tracks over painted surfaces in rock shelters. Offenders include termites (Isoptera) and mudwasps (Hymenoptera), together with mud nests of birds such as the Welcome Swallow *(Hirundo neoxena)* and the Fairy Martin *(Petrocheridon ariel)*. The former is distributed in the southern two-thirds of Australia and the latter is Australia-wide (Slater 1970). The nature of this problem is more fully outlined by Rosenfeld (1985:44-46).

Termite damage to painting sites is generally limited to the northern monsoon area of Australia. A study by Watson and Flood (1987) deals with sites in the Koolburra Plateau near Laura in North Queensland. As with other mud-building organisms, permanent damage is inflicted to pictographs on contact with mud nests and covered runways.

Damage has been observed in rock shelters from animal-induced dust and from animal urine. However, the most common and damaging impact relates to animals coming into direct contact with the images.

Goats are particularly harmful to imagery on rock faces. Rub damage can occur from a height of one metre to ground level and can also be present on walls above ledges. It has a dirty, greasy appearance; there is usually plenty of dung on the floor which is similar in size to sheep dung, but oval shaped rather than spherical. Goat hair and a characteristic goat smell may also provide evidence of the source of damage.

Macropods cause damage in isolated camp spots and this may extend along the wall of the shelter below approximately 300mm in height. It takes a grey to black greasy appearance, but is usually less obvious than that of sheep and goats.

Pigs like to scratch and rub after wallowing in mud; the affected area takes on a dirty or mud-caked appearance from 300 to 600mm above floor height.

Cattle appear to do least damage among the various animals. Walsh (1984:97) described damage to sites in Central Queensland as being confined to low ceilings, sloping wall areas and and protruding sections, mostly a metre or more above floor level.

Buffalos are more of a nuisance; restricted only to northern Australia, these large beasts may rub their muddy sides along the entire length of a shelter. Damage may appear as mud-caked areas of smudged paintings up to two metres above floor height.

Lick damage is caused mainly by feral brumbies and cattle; they lick protected rock faces containing concentrated salts such as soluble chlorides. The problem is well documented by Walsh (1984:94-96), who described engraving sites in the Upper Warrego area of Central Queensland as being almost totally destroyed over a nine year period by this process.

Treatment of damage

It appears that mud-building birds and insects prefer to nest where their predecessors are or have been. Accordingly, the first step in conservation and future prevention is to remove completely all mud nests from these sites. This approach is supported by other workers in the field, including Naumann (1983:179) for the mudwasp *(Sceliphron laetum)* and Watson and Flood (1987:24) for termites. General treatment of this procedure is dealt with by Rosenfeld (1985:64), but in order to complement this material for the fieldworker, two case studies are detailed below. The first documents the removal of bird nests and associated droppings, the second the removal of mudwasp nests.

Removal of nests and droppings of mud-building birds

While the following case study deals specifically with a swallow's nest, the same procedure would apply to the removal of Fairy Martin nests. Mud nests of swallows *(Hirundo neoxena)* were identified as a particular problem at a site in the Adelaide Hills of South Australia where deep, low and dark shelters offer a desirable nesting habitat for this bird. Mud nests are built over images and white droppings cover painted surfaces (Plate 13). In this example the paintings have been executed in red ochre and have a silica skin cover sufficient to allow the site to be washed. The procedure adopted was as follows:

1. The whole mud nest was easily removed by hand, leaving a dry, caked mud surface, most of which was removed using 100mm bristle brushes.

2. A trial area of rock covered by bird droppings was washed using non-ionic detergent ('Lissapol N') and water. The trial area chosen was away from the paintings and at the lowest part of the affected area.

3. With no adverse effects observed immediately following the trial treatment, the washing area was then extended to painted surfaces. Care was taken to observe any deleterious effects especially as the dirty water flowed down over other paintings.

4. The entire area was washed (see Chapter 7: Washing), then lightly sprayed with clean water.

5. The results are shown in Plate 14. Most of the bird droppings were successfully removed, but complete removal in this case would have required heavy scrubbing which would have caused damage to the site.

The mudstains left by the former nest remained. The images in their vicinity were noticeably fainter. Removal of bird droppings from a site without washing has not, to date, been successfully executed.

Removal of mudwasp nests

It is recommended that mudwasp nests be removed from sites because (a) when positioned over paintings they may cause irreversible damage; (b) their presence appears to attract more nests (Naumann 1983:179); (c) old nests break up and may drop dust and organic material onto painted surfaces below.

The procedure for their removal is very simple and generally may be carried out during a routine inspection procedure as demonstrated by the removal of wasp nests at Goonawingal, near Inverell, New South Wales.

At Goonawingal there is a granite boulder site with red pigment paintings on a vertical face. The mudwasp nests were typically located out of human reach on the roof of the shelter in a dry, well-protected part of the site; they were near, but not on top of, the paintings.

During treatment, paintings located directly below the nests were covered with a section of polythene sheet. The operator stood on a ladder and either pulled off the mud nests by hand or knocked them off using the blunt wooden handle of a bronze brush. Most of the mud nest material broke cleanly away from the rock surface and was thrown outside the shelter. Remaining dried mud was then brushed off the rock using a 100mm bristle brush, or a bronze brush for more persistent material. It was neither necessary nor desirable to wash the site.

Approximately forty mud nests were removed in this way, taking a little over an hour to complete the job. Two new wasp nests were removed several years later by a sites officer reinspecting the site and it is necessary in almost every case to monitor and to maintain sites in this way.

Protection against animals

Pest strips

'Shelltox' pest strips contain 186g/kg of dichlorvos, an organophosphate which is slowly released into the air. Watson and Flood (1987:27) have used these, with apparent success, to prevent mudwasp nest-building in shelters in North Queensland. The trial covered a six month period encompassing one nesting season. Similarly, Naumann (1983:173) used pest strips with apparent success at Ubirr, in Kakadu National Park, from November to June.

The main advantage of the pest strips is that no chemical is applied directly to the rock surface. The main disadvantage of the method is that the pest strips need replacing approximately every three months (Naumann 1983:173). The full environmental impact of the toxic chemical dichlorvos is not fully understood.

Termite control

The two possible methods for control of termites outlined by Watson and Flood (1987) are chemical treatment and nest destruction. It is preferable to avoid the use of chemicals on the basis of their toxicity and environmental and occupational health and safety aspects. There are additional problems of ensuring that an absolute chemical barrier is made in order to isolate the painted surface from the soil below. They recommend nest or mound destruction as the most effective method of control. Watson and Flood (1987:24) advised that:

> Earth mounds should be dug out to the depth at which the compactness of chambers characteristic of the central nest gives way to galleries in the soil, the queen should be found and destroyed and the mound material should be broken up and scattered.

Where they occur in an archaeological deposit, appropriate advice should be sought before disturbing earth mounds. Nests in trees should be destroyed within approximately fifty metres of the imagery. Monitoring for reinfestation is further recommended, preferably at the end of the succeeding wet season and then every two or three years. Finally, Watson and Flood recommend that existing termite runways be left undisturbed unless these are threatening to cover hitherto intact areas of pictographs, as newly constructed runways might result and the area of damage be extended.

Bird and insect-proof netting

Exclusion of birds and insects by netting is a feasible prevention method. There are no known Australian examples where this has been implemented.

Animal rubbing stains and stock fencing

There is no known method to date which successfully removes animal stains to reveal intact pictographs. It would appear that this type of damage is permanent. Accordingly, the conservation approach in this area should be one of prevention, by site fencing, rather than cure.

Fencing is the only practical method of preventing animal damage. State authorities should be aware of fence design which must be capable of excluding the animals which are damaging the site. Goat and macropod fences need to be at least two metres high and of sufficiently fine mesh that goats do not get their horns caught. Rosenfeld (personal communication, 1987) observed both struggling and desiccated goats hooked up in fences built in the Cobar area of New South Wales. Cattle fences need to be strongly reinforced with well-anchored corner posts and other supports. Aesthetically it is preferable to bring fences out from the site so as not to interfere with the viewing of the images, and to reduce the visual impact of the fence on the site as a whole. Finally it is important when designing fences to consider the following questions: (a) Will the fence withstand bush fires? (b) Will vegetation growth inside the fence pose a fire hazard to the images? (c) Is there an archaeological deposit present? If so, the fence posts should be placed to avoid it.

6. MANAGING SITES TO REDUCE VISITOR IMPACT

The impact of visitors

The frequency with which visitors touch images is commonly measured by researchers studying visitor behaviour at sites (eg, Gale and Jacobs 1987). Touching includes not only touching with the hand, but also people sitting or standing on surfaces, people's heads or hats touching the painted ceilings of shelters, and people leaning against images when having photographs taken. The introduction of a management facility which reduces the incidence of touching by visitors is regarded as an important contribution to conservation of the images. Hughes (1978:36-41) has documented the fact that the impact of erosion in shelters is accelerated by human contact. Walsh has documented the grease marks which appear on images as the result of people being photographed leaning against a particular spot.

Effects of dust and other airborne materials

The very nature of a deep shelter which affords good protection for the long-term preservation of pictographs often results in a permanently dry floor deposit. Other factors, such as the parent rock material, will determine the percentage of fines (small diameter particles) which constitute the floor deposit. The presence of fine, dry floor material will often result in settlement of fine layers of dust which may be kicked up over pictographs by human or animal visitors. Accumulation of dust can be mitigated by a number of proven management practices (dealt with later in this chapter). Dust layers may obscure or obliterate pictographs, most frequently at the lower levels of a shelter (Plate 15). The problem is further compounded by mineralisation of airborne salts. These can either bond the dust particles to the rock surface or take on the appearance of settled dust. This was the case at a site in Kakadu National Park where management has concentrated upon preventing further dust settlement by restricting vehicle access to the site. John Clarke (personal communication, 1988), who has been studying the site, identified the dust as gypsum and bearing little resemblance to the material on the floor. His interpretation was that the material was derived from the air and this is reinforced by the appearance of the material, which looked like dust.

TREATMENT: To interpret correctly the nature of the problem, it is necessary to have the settling material identified. Whether or not this is known, the alternatives for treating the problem are the same. To date they have resulted only in removing loosely bonded surface material which most likely would have consolidated and added to the exisiting problem if it had remained.

Several methods of removing accumulated airborne materials are outlined below; a combination of these techniques may be appropriate for a particular site.

DRY-BRUSHING: Generally, 100mm bristle brushes are appropriate, worked methodically across the site from top to bottom. Dust cartridge breathing apparatus may need to be worn. In some cases (eg, Arkaroo Rock in South Australia), dry-brushing has caused surface material to adhere to the rock face, leaving an unsightly sheen. In this instance it was preferable to wash the affected part of the site.

COMPRESSED AIR: Where dry-brushing is not successful or appropriate, compressed air has been used; it is important to work downward from the affected area.

LONG-FIBRE TISSUE: Schwartzbaum (personal commmunication, 1985) described a method of washing water soluble pigments through long-fibre tissue paper (Appendix 1). Several wet layers of this material are laid over the water-sensitive pigment. A wet bristle brush may then be worked into the paper, which absorbs surface dirt or loosely bonded graffiti. The method is slow but can be applied to sites which otherwise may not be washed.

WASHING: The site may be washed following the same procedure as for graffiti removal (see below).

Vandalism

This universal problem will, no doubt, continue to haunt the site manager. There are two approaches. Firstly, direct site conservation techniques can be used to remove, lessen or obscure the visual impact of drawn, painted and engraved graffiti. Secondly, management and education can be used to mitigate its further occurrence. It is strongly emphasised that a double-edged approach, involving both site conservation and appropriate visitor management, must be instigated simultaneously to overcome the problem of vandalism at Aboriginal sites.

Management of visitors

The site manager has a number of options in dealing with visitation. These are: to do nothing; to restrict access; to create signs which direct visitors; to provide a visitors' book for comments; and to place interpretative material on site. Other options are to restrict access to guided tours and to erect human barriers such as mesh screening, low guidance fencing or barriers, footpaths or boardwalks.

Details of each of these options are given below, in order to provide specifications for site managers, together with an outline of the purpose which is served by each. Having in mind that sites can be categorised in terms of their significance and levels of visitation, a range of appropriate management options may be recommended for each category.

There is a misconception among site managers that developed, high-visitation sites are sacrificed to tourism to protect other sites. Studies and observations by Gale and Jacobs (1983:40), suggest that the continual presence of visitors appears to limit damage because overt acts of vandalism tend to occur when no one else is around; there appears to be a point at which increasing visitation will reduce acts of vandalism by self-regulation.

Restricting access

There are several places where high-visitation sites have been selected for development as 'tourist sites' and at the same time, managers have attempted to reduce levels of visitation at the remaining, undeveloped sites.

This practice is not always successful, however, particularly near more populated areas where a high proportion of visitors are local. Attempts were made near Gosford, New South Wales, to divert visitors from a famous complex of petroglyphs known as the Feast Group, to a nearby developed site known as Bulgandry. The track to the undeveloped Feast Group was partly obscured and allowed to overgrow. Routed signs encouraged visitors towards the developed Bulgandry site. Despite this, the Feast Group continues to receive levels of visitation sufficient to cause vandalism; in addition, visitors continue to clear the access track to the site.

A successful case is described by Walsh (1983:11-12) at Carnarvon Gorge, Queensland, where three main undeveloped galleries were receiving high levels of visitation. Two of these were chosen for visitor development by the construction of boardwalks together with other forms of promotion such as the production of brochures providing site interpretation. At the third site, visitation was successfully discouraged by (a) deleting all references to the site from maps and written material; (b) avoiding public acknowledgement of the site's existence; (c) camouflaging the access track to allow natural revegetation of the former entry point.

Restricting information

Restriction of site information, particularly regarding location details of isolated sites, remains one of the best protective measures against visitor related site deterioration. Discretion rests entirely with site managers and site registrars. This practice appears to be common throughout Australia.

Visitors' books

It is generally accepted that the visitors' book serves two purposes. Firstly, it redirects vandalism from the site to the book and, secondly, it may provide information to both the visitor and the manager. K Sullivan (1984:52-53) has provided detailed guidelines for drawing up and maintaining visitors' books in sites:

> The underlying principle is that the condition of the visitors' book affects people's attitudes to it. Some sort of regular maintenance is therefore essential. Depending on the frequency of visitors, this could vary from once a year to once every five years. If more regular maintenance proves necessary, other management strategies may need to be considered.
>
> 1. Some form of protection, from dust, animals or water, is needed. A plastic bag may be adequate .... .
> 2. The book should be hard covered and in strong binding. It is useful if the binding allows removal of discrete segments without destroying the book, as people tend to remove a small number of pages for use as toilet paper, for notes, and so on.
> 3. Experience has shown that it is important that the pages be ruled up, and headed: Date, Name, Address, with the opposing page headed Comments.
> 4. The books should contain information about the site. A plan of the site and discussion of its most interesting features is recommended. Other general information about sites and site protection can be included in the back of the book, together with the address of the nearest Service office and Aboriginal Lands Council. The books discussed have all been done by hand, in motel rooms with limited equipment. While it would be useful to have books professionally printed with ruled pages and headings, and some standard information, each site requires some individual information. Site specific features can be inserted by hand in the field. The 'handmade' quality of the books would appear to be appreciated by visitors who have commented upon it and who feel it indicates 'loving care'.
> 5. Because the condition of the book is so important and because visits to the sites will be infrequent, on the spot maintenance is important. The following is a list of

suggested equipment to have handy: glue, sticky tape, paper, staples, ruler, scissors, pencils, pens, rubber, white-out, plastic bags. These things are necessary for mending/strengthening the book, cleaning the book, and making any alterations necessary. Sometimes one discovers that something originally written about the site is misleading or having an undesired effect, and it may need to be removed or altered.

Removal of graffiti in the book ... should not be done automatically. Books do get grubby and sometimes children scribble. Erasers and white-out are useful to help keep the book looking cared for.

Deliberately offensive comments, either racist or obscene, are another matter. One reason why the book is there is to allow a venue for this expression other than the site itself.

Further, ... other visitors who dislike it react by commenting upon it and a peer group pressure of comment builds up in the book. In some cases, removal of graffiti from the book may well lead to an angry and dangerous reaction should the authors return. A balance between caring for the book, and a venue for free expression must be kept.

Signs and printed materials

Signs placed at sites can be either official or interpretative. Each serve their own purpose.

The function of offical signs is to give some sort of official presence. They are applicable particularly to isolated significant heritage sites. People coming across a site in an isolated area feel some right of ownership; graffiti to record this 'first' visit, or pilferage of moveable material may result. An official sign reveals that the site is both known and visited by the authorities. A second function (as with visitors' books) is to redirect vandalism from the site to the sign. Vandals appear to gain satisfaction by striking at officialdom; accordingly, signs should be placed in a visible location but sufficiently distant from the imagery that they do not interfere with photography.

On-site interpretative signs vary significantly in content and design. Fay Gale (personal communication, 1987), during a survey and interview of visitors to sites in the Sydney district, recommended that sign content be site-specific. General site information tends to be misleading and visitors' needs are most satisfied by information which tells them specifically what they are looking at and something about it.

While it is difficult to formulate a general recipe for interpretative signs, studies by Gale and Jacobs (1987:91-92) indicate that more people read signs which (a) contain few words, (b) contain photos, and (c) are well-located.

For example, more people were likely to read detailed signs located at a car park rather than those placed en route to or at the actual site destination. When the sign was located at the site it was important to the visitors that it did not obstruct the view, particularly for photography. With regard to sign content, visitors were found to appreciate signs which were site-specific.

It would seem that the range in age and background of people visiting sites is so variable that it is not easy to provide a single leaflet which would satisfy the needs of all. Accordingly, the greater the range of material, either free or saleable, the better. It is generally considered that information needs to be available to visitors and distributed at some point near the site. Furthermore, if printed leaflets are to be distributed on site, they need to be site-specific. However, this practice sometimes results in brochures littering the site which then requires regular maintenance (I Webb, personal communication, 1986). Elsewhere, this has not been reported as a problem. For example, an experiment was conducted by Gale and Jacobs (1987:93) in which brochures were handed personally to visitors at Nourlangie Rock in Kakadu National Park and at two sites in the Flinders Ranges. None of these brochures were thrown away and, in all three cases, were found to modify visitor behaviour at the site in a positive way and generally to enhance the experience of the visitor. However, care must be exercised in interpreting these findings, as the effect of personal distribution of brochures may well have influenced the visitors' conduct by giving greater value to the brochure than if it were self-dispensed.

It is likely that all workers in this field have at some stage been moved by the ambience of a site, impressed by its antiquity, or the design and meaning of figures present. The most difficult task is to get these impressions across to the public. It is considered that it is necessary to put more effort into interpreting the images simply because this is what the visiting public need to stimulate their caring interest. Clegg (1983:89) related an instructive and humorous instance where, in frustration, he made up a mythical story about a site successfully to stimulate the flagging interest of a group of tourists. While no one is suggesting we take interpretation this far, Aboriginal consultation combined with the knowledge which is available regarding weapons, picture style and recurring figures, for example, can provide the basis for legitimate interpretation of the images. Gillespie (1983:26-27) argued the need for a more

Aboriginal-oriented interpretation, moving away from the more traditional European 'art gallery' practice.

At a more basic management level, Walsh (1983:12-13) made some very relevant points regarding interpretation and printed material at Carnarvon Gorge, Queensland:

> Rock art does not necessarily have to be visually spectacular to attract sincere interest from the public, and yet in instances even 'great' art may initially appear unimpressive and uninteresting to an uninformed visiting public. Experience has highlighted the fact that most visitors have developed firm, preconceived ideas of just what the rock art will be, long before reaching the site. Such anticipation is rarely satiated, and in many instances visitors express feelings of disappointment at the 'anticlimax' after first visual contact with the art.
>
> ... . This feeling can, for the greater part, be attributed to the almost total lack of understanding of both the motifs, and their significance prevailing amongst the general public. It is probably that similar 'anticlimax' feeling that would be evident in 'non art-oriented' members of the public visiting commercial art galleries which feature art works other than the traditional portrait/landscape themes.
>
> The solution to this problem lies in basic interpretation and education, two aspects consistently underrated and given too low a priority in site management programs. ...
>
> Responsibility certainly rests with the controlling authority to provide adequate basic interpretative material, but encouragement should be given to private or commercial operations to prepare the more expensive quality publications. Support and technical assistance with the preparation of such material ensures a finished product complementary to the ideology and image of the controlling authority. Such an arrangement greatly assists the authority with the fulfilment of its obligations and serves a number of purposes:
>
> 1. Assures availability of a wide range of interpretative/ educational material for members of the public.
> 2. Permits the production of high quality material which controlling authorities could otherwise seldom afford to publish.
> 3. Frees authorities from the burden of often heavy costs in both time and capital outlay associated with compilation and publication of such a range of material.
>
> Another significant point is provision for the distribution of such material. Little value

can be gained if such publications are only available at a distant point, perhaps hundreds of kilometres from the actual art sites. Serious consideration should be given by controlling authorities to the merits of retailing assistance through permit offices and interpretation centres. Values derived from on-site availability of such officially sanctioned quality material are not to be underestimated. The resultant man-hour savings in personalised interpretation more than compensates for the minor inconveniences associated with such sales.

Guided tours

I have observed guided tours of Aboriginal sites in operation in several states. The most intensive guided tour system in operation in Australia is at Kakadu National Park. A free tour operator training course is run by the Australian National Parks and Wildlife Service at the beginning of each tourist season; this greatly assists with the education of tour operators in the correct form of behaviour at sites and gives them accurate facts and information for later use. Gale and Jacobs (1987:46) demonstrated the disadvantages of poorly guided tours which frequently result in a high level of touching of imagery by tour group visitors, with operators providing either incorrect information or no information at all. The results of unsatisfactory tour guiding suggest that the relevant state authorities are obligated to either regulate or educate private tour operators who visit Aboriginal sites.

In addition to commercial tours, several national parks authorities run seasonal guided tours of sites, which generally provide a high standard of tour information and conduct. In New South Wales, seasonal ranger programs are funded by the state's National Parks Foundation, a fund-raising organisation.

Mesh screening

The term 'mesh screening' has been used to refer to the person-proof steel mesh grills which have been erected at many sites in Australia. These generally consist of galvanised steel mesh fixed to a galvanised pipe frame which is in turn fixed across the cave entrance. They restrict visitor entry to the site and usually contain locked gates.

The visual impact of mesh grills on the site is their most striking disadvantage (Plates 16 and 17). However, this should be weighed against the fact that the structure can later be removed with little impact to the site provided installation and positioning is carefully considered. Damage to floor deposit has been reported in Victoria and South Australia following the installation of mesh screens. Construction and installation costs are invariably high.

In all cases mesh screens have been built in shelters which are thought to contain significant sites under visitor threat, either close to centres of population such as Sydney or in remote areas subject to tourism such as the Grampians in Victoria. In most cases the sites selected have already been vandalised by graffiti. In all cases the mesh screens have prevented further graffiti from occurring over pictographs, although one example of shotgun damage is present in Bull Cave, near Campbelltown, New South Wales. Continued graffiti outside the mesh screen has been observed in New South Wales, Victoria and South Australia.

Guidance fencing, barriers and walkways

Low barriers at sites have been observed by workers such as Gale (1984) as being very effective at guiding visitors through sites. By comparison with other structures they are cheap yet still effective. They may take the form of wooden fences, or chain or rope barriers which, although easily climbed, present a psychological line which clearly should not be crossed. Without this official line, it seems to visitors that there are no behavioural standards or limits presented, and that it is acceptable to touch, rub or pick at the images.

A study by Gale and Jacobs (Gale 1984) at Ubirr in Kakadu National Park clearly demonstrated the value of effective visitor signs, boardwalks and barriers. The area was first studied in June 1982 when paths had been marked out clearly but there were no fences, barriers, on-site signs or interpretation at any of the individual pictograph sites. At this time some twenty-one per cent of visitors were observed to have touched the images, and one person was observed deliberately vandalising. A year later, when the visitor management material had been put in place, only one person out of 611 was observed touching the images.

Many paths and boardwalks have now been constructed at Australian sites. Their function is to display the imagery clearly to a large number of visitors with the least possible impact resulting to the site. Without having to step off the boardwalk, visitors must be able to view and photograph the images clearly. Consultation with Aboriginal custodians must take place before such structures are built as in some cases planned structures could give offence to site custodians.

Four case studies of walkways

Like most site structures in Australia, boardwalks have been constructed on a trial and error basis. Managers have perceived the need for some form of walkway and have used the knowledge and information available at the time in an attempt to build the most suitable structure for a particular site. We are now in a position to look at various examples, and after studies by Gale (1984), an evaluation can be made with regard to practical structural, aesthetic and safety aspects of designs and construction. Accordingly, several case studies are dealt with below with the intention of drawing out suitable guidelines for managers involved in future boardwalk construction.

1. Mootwingee (near Broken Hill, New South Wales)

To my knowledge this was the first walkway constructed in an Australian site, being substantially completed in July 1978 (Plate 18). Visitors were meant to be conducted to the petroglyph site by guided tour, so no signposting or interpretative material was incorporated into the project. The design was drawn up principally by the New South Wales Public Works Department, whose emphasis was on public safety at the expense of aesthetic considerations. (The site is no longer open to the public.) Partly because this was the first attempt, a number of mistakes were made both before and during construction. However, several useful lessons have been learnt from this experience:

1. The walkway is no longer in use principally because of objections to visitation by the Local Aboriginal Land Council. At the time of construction procedures for Aboriginal consultation were not in place and this result was unforeseen.
2. The design of the walkway, with hand rails etc, succeeded in keeping visitors off the site.
3. The siting of the walkway did not allow visitors to view or photograph the entire site but merely a sample of it.
4. The material used was prefabricated metal which did not blend well with the natural setting of the site.
5. There was no local supervision during construction because of staff problems in the area at the time. As a result, a number of mistakes were made such as mixing concrete on part of the site and the impairment of site drainage in the placement of concrete footings.

It should be remembered that this was the first walkway constructed; there were no other examples to draw upon and these defects were obvious only after construction. Nevertheless, considerable forethought was put into the project, particularly regarding aspects of public safety and prefabrication, in order to reduce the working time and hence the impact on the site.

2. Carnarvon Gorge, Central Queensland

This case study of boardwalk construction in a large shelter containing vast areas of pictographs and petroglyphs (Plate 19) has been provided by Walsh (1983). Additional considerations here were problems of dust, resulting from heavy visitation, combined with the extremely soft, friable precipice sandstone on which the images were stencilled and engraved. Walsh wrote (1983:5–7):

> Extensive on-site discussion and planning by local ranger staff resulted in a basic layout plan. In order to be effective the completed development must adequately fulfil the majority of the needs of the visiting public, particularly with respect to both viewing and photographing the various art panels. Experiments were carried out, using both 35mm and medium format cameras with various lenses, eventually determining the most suitable walkway positioning for photographic purposes. Tests were carried out at the proposed elevated level of the boardwalks, ensuring that distances to overhanging art surfaces were adequate to avoid touch. Key vantage points were selected to establish observation points superior to those available from site floor viewing. Resting positions appointed with adequate seating facilities were planned at strategic positions. These provided commanding views of significant art panels without interfering with normal pedestrian traffic. Consultations and on-site inspections with geologists determined areas of possible instability, particularly in the overhanging ceiling areas. Walkway positions were accordingly altered to avoid any possible risk.

3. Main Gallery, Ubirr, Kakadu National Park

This case study is fully detailed by Gillespie (1983:24); it presents the additional factor of Aboriginal consultation. Uncontrolled visitor access had led to damage to paintings on lower rock faces, together with dust problems and damage to floor deposits. A boardwalk, designed by the Department of Housing and Construction, initially appeared to cater adequately to the site and its problems. Following discussions with senior custodians of the site, the boardwalk was ultimately rejected. In its place a walkway through the site made of local sandstone was selected. A route of minimum site disturbance was chosen in compromise with the optimum route for viewing the figures.

In Gillespie's view, some progress had been made in satisfying the public's desire to view the paintings, and the custodians had participated in decisions concerning the management of their heritage.

4. Bulgandry, near Gosford, New South Wales

A low-level boardwalk was constructed on a petroglyph site at Bulgandry to cater for the public demand to view Sydney engravings. The site was chosen because the figures were considered relatively visible and because the site was located near a public road. There was an additional advantage that visitors might be diverted to this site away from a nearby petroglyph site known as the Feast Group, which is generally more difficult to see and considered more significant in terms of the number and style of figures present. Several additional points can be noted about the design and construction of this boardwalk: (a) It was designed to be built with local timber, ironbark, which was left to weather for several months to leach out any tannins or resins which might have stained the rock surface. (b) Construction was supervised by a ranger with a longstanding interest in and respect for the site and who also contributed to the design of the walkway. (c) An interpretative package, including a site pamphlet and on-site interpretative signs were added to give general district site information.

Following a visitor survey by Gale and Jacobs in 1987, these observations were reported: (a) Approximately thirty per cent of visitors were leaving the walkway and walking over the site; Gale and Jacobs recommended that a low barrier be constructed to try to prevent this. (b) The generalised nature of the interpretative signs tended to confuse visitors (some looking under the walkway for the paintings), who had little idea about what they were looking at. This finding confirms the necessity for site-specific interpretation when information is displayed on site. (c) Sydney engravings are typically difficult to recognise, and vandalism, in the form of scratching-in and outlining figures, had occurred; what had been clearly visible petroglyphs to the trained eye were not so visible to the general public. As a result of continuing vandalism, highlighting of engravings was undertaken (Chapter 7).

Guidelines for construction of walkways

In view of the results of these case studies these recommendations are made concerning walkway construction:

1. Consultation with Aboriginal custodians should take place at an early stage, allowing the flexibility to modify completely the design, or withdraw altogether.

2. Wherever possible, all figures must be clear and able to be photographed adequately from the walkway with a setback sufficient to prevent visitors touching the images.

3. Construction work must be supervised by permanent staff with a long-term interest in the site.

4. Materials used should complement the aesthetics of the site. Experience has shown that the use of local natural materials adds to the appeal and practicality of the structure. In many cases it has also reduced the cost of the project.

5. Safety aspects require professional consultation.

6. A visitor-oriented approach to the site, as demonstrated in the Carnarvon Gorge example, is an important consideration.

7. Modification of the design after installation and evaluation of visitor use should be anticipated, as has been the case at Bulgandry.

8. A barrier limiting and defining the area where visitors are permitted to go should be incorporated into the design of the structure.

9. It is necessary to include interpretation which is specific to the site, in order to provide protection to the site and to enhance the visitors' experience. This is becoming accepted visitor management practice.

Site categories and management strategies

Having considered the various management options (signs, screens, walkways), the site manager is faced with the necessity of determining which of these are suitable for a particular site. Broadly, there are three fundamental factors which, in most cases, will determine a suitable site management strategy:

Heritage significance to Aboriginal people
Heritage significance generally
Visitation levels

Heritage significance to Aboriginal people is an independent and overriding factor, which dictates that any management strategy must be in accordance with the wishes or recommendations of the relevant community and, particularly, the traditional custodians where these can be identified. An otherwise appropriate management strategy may not be applicable because of Aboriginal views concerning the cultural significance of a place.

In order to determine guidelines for appropriate management strategies within this framework, it is appropriate to categorise sites by formulating a simple matrix combining site heritage significance with visitation levels. By categorising sites in this way, suitable management strategies may then be indicated, as outlined below.

Table 1.	Site categories: Heritage significance and visitation level
	Heritage significance
A	Very significant or rare site. Generally recognised as having high heritage values of national importance; on Register of the National Estate.
B	Site of regional or local importance.
C	Representative site.
	Visitation level
1.	High
2.	Medium
3.	Low

Thus a site category A/3 would be considered an important site with a low level of visitation; C/2 would be a simple, representative site with medium visitation, and so on.

Table 2 summarises management recommendations for each of the categories of site outlined above. In each case, appropriate Aboriginal consultation is assumed.

A thematic approach to site promotion and development

As the above table indicates, development of sites may be necessary to accommodate increasing levels of visitation. Without the application of foresight and planning principles the site manager can easily fall into the trap of *ad hoc* development purely on the basis of past visitor pressure. A more structured planning approach is necessary and Sullivan (1985) suggests that an overview of various themes be presented within a given region in order to give the visitor a full and coherent story of Aboriginal life and at the same time prevent needless repetition of interpretative material. This example of thematic treatment of New South Wales prehistory is taken from Sullivan (1985: 20).

By starting with this broad thematic list, the site manager may focus on two or three particular themes which are representative of Aboriginal prehistory for a given region, then select suitable sites for visitor development and promotion.

Table 2.	Recommended management strategies
Site Category	**Recommended Management Strategies**
A/3	Sign and visitors' book placed at the site in an inconspicuous position so as not to draw attention to the site.
C/2 C/3	With present and predicted staffing levels in Australia, management is by sporadic official visitation and/or by public informants.
B/2 B/3 B/1*	Visitors' book and sign. When significant damage occurs or is anticipated, consider mesh screening.
A/1 A/2 B/1* C/1	Walkway and/or low guidance fencing or rope/chain barriers, together with site-specific interpretative signs, guided tours.

*Note: B/1 has two alternative but appropriate strategies.

Table 3	Thematic treatment of New South Wales prehistory
Theme	**Sites**
CULTURAL CHANGE AND CONTINUITY	Sites which show occupancy over a long period—occupation deposits which have been researched.
ECONOMIC AND ENVIRONMENTAL ADAPTATION	Occupation sites, middens, food remains etc.
TECHNOLOGY	Stone quarries, grinding grooves, fish traps, canoe trees, and other artefacts.
ART AND RELIGION	Paintings, engravings, stone arrangements ceremonial grounds.
SOCIETY	Camp sites, trading sites, ceremonial sites.
ABORIGINAL/WHITE CONTACT	Mission sites, massacre sites, nineteenth century pastoral properties, etc.
CONTEMPORARY ABORIGINAL LIFE	Sites of Aboriginal political activities. Aboriginal art and craft shops and displays.

7. SITE VANDALISM AND VISITOR IMPACT

Types of vandalism

Vandalism in sites takes several forms and it is necessary for the conservator or site manager to categorise and look at the underlying reasons for it. Most graffiti can be removed with varying degrees of damage to the site being incurred, but graffiti removal must be accompanied by an appropriate management strategy catering to the specific situation and developed with consideration of its causes.

Vandalism may take the form of graffiti, highlighting of figures by scratching or chalking where figures are difficult to see, inflicted damage such as shooting, 'souveniring', and accidental or inquisitive touching of images. Where conservation work is carried out at sites, it is imperative that this work be immediately followed by appropriate management strategies as previously outlined, otherwise vandalism will simply continue, thus negating any conservation work carried out.

Graffiti comes in a variety of shapes, sizes and materials such as paints, dyes, charcoal, chalk, crayon, scratching and engraving. There are several ways to remove and mitigate its impact and these methods are discussed below.

Removal of graffiti

Information on practical aspects of graffiti removal has been requested by staff in most states. Accordingly, a comprehensive coverage of this problem is given.

Removing significant amounts of graffiti from a site, particularly old graffiti, should not be attempted by anyone without previous experience. Graffiti removal is frequently practised in New South Wales, and on-site training would be available to any site manager by simply being an extra hand on a scheduled field trip there. Very fresh graffiti on an otherwise unvandalised site is an entirely different matter. In such cases, the site manager should consider its immediate removal either by following the steps outlined below or seeking further advice.

Preliminary considerations

ABORIGINAL CONSULTATION: Graffiti removal involves touching and handling the site. This practice may be objectionable to Aboriginal people responsible for the site. Wherever possible, consultation with Aboriginal custodians should be a prerequisite to graffiti removal.

SITE RECORDING: Graffiti is often drawn using materials such as charcoal which if not entirely removed may be later confused with the original imagery. It is therefore necessary to record the site fully before taking remedial action. The practice adopted in New South Wales is to record the original imagery and the graffiti using clear polythene on which the former is directly recorded in one colour and the graffiti in another (Plate 21). A problem recognised with this method of recording is the storage and retrieval of information. Presently, the most efficient way of doing this is to reduce the scale of the 1:1 polythene sheet recording by photography from which accurate scale reduction drawings can be made should this be necessary.

Where graffiti is obvious, annotated black and white photography is sufficient for recording purposes, black and white being chosen for archival stability.

TIMELY REMOVAL: Very recent graffiti, when it is in materials such as charcoal, chalk and some paints, is much more simply removed than older graffiti. In cases where sites are closely managed and where they are otherwise free of vandalism, the procedure recommended is to remove the graffiti without further ado using the techniques outlined below.

POST-CONTACT IMAGES: Drawings of a typical style could be considered an integral part of the site. In such cases it is often a good idea to consult others before removing these figures. Plate 22 gives an example of what an increasing number of researchers consider to be post-contact imagery, be it Aboriginal or European. This assessment is based purely on style. Therefore, the general policy is, when in doubt, don't remove.

HISTORIC GRAFFITI: Historic graffiti may take the form of either names, initials or drawings. It is generally agreed that names or initials of early explorers should stay, although there is often doubt as to their authenticity. Early settlers generally do not rank quite as highly and are placed in a 'grey' area as to whether or not they should be removed. It is wise to consult recognised historians, particularly local historians, in order to make an adequate assessment.

An example which serves to highlight the dilemma faced by the conservator is a site at Nullo Mountain near Rylestone, New South Wales. In this instance the national park district superintendent requested that graffiti be removed from the site and an inspection and report was made accordingly. Two rather nicely drawn horses were present and it was proposed to remove both (Plates 23 and 24). As it happened, in the period between submitting the report and doing the job, the local ranger had by chance made contact with a local historian who advised that one of the figures was allegedly drawn by a well-known bushranger who lived in the shelter for some time. It was said that the second horse was a recent copy and had no historical significance. Accordingly, the alleged copy together with numerous other names and initials were removed and the reputed historic drawing of the horse remained. This was the decision of the day and remains open to criticisms varying from the advocacy of total removal of non-Aboriginal figures to the opposite view that no images, including initials, should have been removed from this site.

Assessment

As the instance above demonstrates, it is preferable on larger graffiti removal jobs to inspect the site, make a brief report with photos, and circulate your intentions within the organisation and locally before carrying out the work.

During the first inspection these steps are important:

1. Photograph the site, preferably using black and white film which may be archived. Additional colour prints or slides may be useful for reports. Photography will provide a before-and-after record.

2. Make a note of the materials used to draw the graffiti and equipment which will be required, such as ladders, etc.

3. Estimate the time that it will take to do the job and the number of people required.

4. Test the removal techniques proposed on a small area of the site away from the imagery, particularly for the most common form of graffiti present.

Cleaning a site

The procedure for cleaning starts in the same way whether or not it is intended to wash the site. Washing is simply the last step which results in a more thorough and complete removal of graffiti.

DRY-BRUSHING: Dry-brushing is used to remove dry pigment graffiti such as chalk and charcoal.

1. Start by using clean bristle brushes (50mm is a good size).

2. Select a small area to begin with and observe very closely the effect which brushing has, both on the graffiti and the original pictures. If original pigment is being removed by this process, then stop. In this case it will only be possible to remove that graffiti not drawn directly over the original images. It will also be necessary to use finer brushes over which more precision can be exercised when working close to the pictographs. It will be out of the question to consider washing such figures.

3. If unacceptable levels of smudging of graffiti is occurring and the site is not to be washed, then do not work over the top of pictographs, and use finer brushes where graffiti occurs close to the imagery, with more precise brushing.

4. An electrically-driven jeweller's handpiece with replaceable nylon brush discs is recommended for this purpose (Appendix 1 has specifications). The brush has a track width of approximately 4mm and, being electrically driven, allows the user considerably more precision than manual techniques. A potentiometer fitted to the unit allows speed to be varied between 0 and 25,000rpm; the setting most commonly used is around 7,000rpm. Care must be taken not to press hard onto the rock surface. Heat thus generated tends to melt the nylon bristles, leaving a black mark on the rock surface. Again, it is imperative to observe continually the effect which the brushing is having.

5. Experiment first on a local, non-image-bearing rock away from the site until the technique has been mastered.

The results obtained using the nylon brushes are generally most satisfactory and their use is highly recommended. The main disadvantage with the system is that it also requires a lightweight power generator which must be carried to the site. A thirty metre extension lead is also used in order to separate the associated noise and fumes from the site working environment (Appendix 1).

FIBREGLASS BRUSHES: The use of fibreglass brushes has been described by Clarke (1978:90):

> These brushes are used for jewellery cleaning and consist of a large number of glass fibres bound with string, the largest size (15mm dia x 150mm) are the most suitable. They can be obtained from wholesale watchmakers' supply shops. With the brush it is possible to remove the offending pigment with a scrubbing action (we have even been able to remove charcoal graffiti off the top of Aboriginal paintings without causing any

damage). The method works because the glass fibres, while being harder and stiffer than normal brushes, are still softer than most rock-forming minerals so there is no scratching of the surface. The method is rather slow if a large area is to be cleaned, and a large number of brushes will be required since they wear out quickly. The brushes release numerous small fibres which can cause skin irritation so protective clothes and mask should be used.

Since publication of the method in 1978 two disadvantages have been observed. Firstly, the brushes are difficult to obtain; they must be ordered in bulk and imported by the one known supplier (Appendix 1). Secondly, the risk to the user's health of fine fibreglass particles becoming lodged in the lungs should be taken seriously; so much so that I strongly recommend against their continued use. However, if they are used, well-fitting dust masks should always be worn. (Paper masks do not prevent inhalation of very fine fibres; a cartridge-type respirator will.)

PARTICLE BLASTING OR AIR BRUSHING: To date, the limited experimentation with this technique has shown it to be impractical or with limited application for graffiti removal in Australia. The use of air brushes is, however, said to have had successful application overseas (Schwartzbaum, personal communication, 1985). The method uses an air compressor and gun which directs particles onto the rock face. Softer particles such as dolomite or glass beads are less likely to scratch the rock surface. While the method may have considerable potential, more experimentation is required before it can be recommended. Particle blasting was used to remove old paint situated well away from pictographs at Nullo Mountain in New South Wales. Breathing apparatus is essential as a health requirement.

WASHING: Following dry-brushing, a more satisfactory result may be obtained if it is possible to wash the site. Graffiti can be removed more completely and loose dust and micro-organic material covering the images can be removed at the same time. Assessment of whether a site can be washed or not is somewhat subjective and open to debate. It depends upon the degree to which and manner in which the pigments are bonded to the rock surface. It is common for surface mineralisation to develop over painted surfaces, and the degree of mineralisation will determine whether the site can be washed without removing pigment or altering its morphology. Certainly, if freshly painted or drawn pictographs were washed, an unacceptable quantity of pigment would be removed. In addition, the morphology of the pigment may be significantly altered, resulting in pigment migration or features such as run-marks forming, or loss of surface brush markings, for example.

The first thing to look for is whether or not the site ever naturally becomes wet. Signs of direct water erosion displayed by figure cutting (Chapter 1) or salt deposits marking the edge of water seepage lines (Plates 1 and 2) are the most common indicators. Secondly, look for evidence of surface mineralisation which most commonly takes the form of a low milky sheen over the imagery. The lustre of the pigment is important in this assessment. A pigment with a flat, powdery lustre should not be considered for washing. Ideally, sample examination under a scanning electron microscope would yield a more positive identification but presently, given the level of most state budgets, this is not a practical consideration.

If, after the above examination, the site is considered suitable for washing, the next step is to select a small trial area for testing, preferably in an obscure part of the site. The final consideration before starting is to avoid washing the entire site. There are two main reasons for this. Firstly, washing has a potentially high impact on a site. Certainly it rates higher than touching, a practice for which we criticise others. Accordingly, washing should be kept to the minimum area necessary to achieve the desired purpose. The second reason is to retain washed and unwashed sections of the shelter for future comparison. In this way, any long-term effects can be observed. Also, sites which require conservation work are often badly damaged. A question often asked when revisiting such sites is whether the figures were previously as faint or whether it is a result of past conservation work. In such cases it is very reassuring to be able to point to areas of the site which have not been touched, and can be directly compared with areas where graffiti has been removed.

The method currently used was developed and described by John Clarke (1978:90). It can be summarised as follows:

1. Divide the area of the site to be washed into sections. Each section should be approximately two metres square.
2. Start from the top of each section, one at a time, and work methodically downwards.
3. Use clean or deionised water with no additives. Alternatively a detergent solution consisting of 1:2,000 (5ml to 10 litres of water) of 'Lissapol N' (non-ionic detergent; see Appendix 1) may be brushed onto each area, using a clean bristle brush (50 to 100mm). The solution is worked up into a thick froth where graffiti occurs.
4. Limit this activity to the graffiti contained within each area, then lightly

but thoroughly spray the area down, working from top to bottom with clean water. A clean twenty litre knapsack spray is useful for this purpose.

5. Where graffiti is not located over the imagery, the water or detergent process may be repeated.

6. Where necessary, use progressively harder brushes, conventional scrubbing brushes or bronze brushes (used for cleaning suede). Steel wire brushes may be used in extreme cases but should be avoided as they will mark the rock surface. The general rule is to use the softest fibre brush which will achieve the desired result. Only pigments which are strongly bonded to the rock by surface mineralisation may be scrubbed in this way.

REMOVING WAX OR WATERPROOF CRAYONS AND PAINT: Wax crayons are made from paraffin wax with a coloured pigment added. There are two effective methods of removing wax from rock surfaces.

1. In areas which can be washed lightly, run clean water over the affected area and simultaneously brush the graffiti using a bronze brush (two people are required). The wax crayon will float off in small chunks, leaving no residue (Plate 25). At engraving sites where dark micro-organic material is growing on the surface, the freshly treated area may appear distinctly clean and lighter in colour. In such cases the former rock colour has been restored naturally within six months.

2. Apply a cotton wool poultice soaked with toluene, or sepiolite. This method is detailed by Clarke (1978:90). On exposed rock surfaces solvents will evaporate very quickly, often before they have had time to dissolve the offending material. Clarke recommends the use of kerosene in such cases, combined with a black polythene sheet placed over the work to slow the evaporation rate. I have always succeeded using bronze brushes and water. The organic solvents used in the second method are partly absorbed by the rock, sending the coloured wax deeper into the rock fabric and leaving behind the coloured stain of the wax crayon which was only partly removed. This is particularly so when treating Hawkesbury Sandstone.

To remove paint from washable sites, the method described by Clarke (1978:89) is recommended:

Where feasible, paint should be removed as soon as possible from rock surfaces as exposure to sunlight and high temperatures can cause polymer cross-linking and other changes which make the paint even more difficult to remove.

After trying many of the normally used solvents, we have found that two brand name commercial paint removers are more effective and more practical to use. These products, 'Berger Strip' and 'Poly Stripper', consist of a methylene chloride base with xylene and a gelling agent. They can therefore be applied to vertical or overhanging surfaces. They do not evaporate as rapidly as pure liquid solvents.

In normal circumstances the paint stripper is applied by brush to the paint only, and allowed to act for fifteen minutes. The treated area is then scrubbed with a strong non-ionic detergent solution in water (5ml 'Lissapol N' in 10ml water), until a thick froth is built up on the rock surface. The whole area is then washed with clean water. The procedure will often need to be repeated several times to remove all paint.

In most cases a paint brush is used for the scrubbing, but on hard, coarse textured rocks, it may be necessary to use a wire brush. This is only done in extreme cases as there is a risk of scratching the rock surface; it is preferable to leave minor traces of paint on the rock than to damage the surface. Moreover, wire-brushing is not normally carried out when removing graffiti which overlies original imagery.

We have used the above technique to remove vandals' paint from on top of red pigmented Aboriginal paintings without damage to the paintings.

There are several precautions to be taken when using this technique:

- Methylene chloride, which burns the skin, must be used with caution;
- Protective clothing, gloves and a face mask are necessary;
- The site must be well ventilated.

Both the paint remover and detergent will remove lichen from rock surfaces, as well as dust and dirt, and this will cause a clean patch in the area treated. In one case, we removed a large painted name from the entrance to a rock shelter only to find the name still present as a silhouette of lichen-free rock. White rock art pigments are easily disrupted by organic solvents and should be avoided when using this method.

No successful technique has been developed for removal of paint over the top of pictographs which cannot be washed. Where paint has been applied adjacent to but not directly over them, a successful method used was to shield the images using a polythene sheet taped to the rock surface. The exposed painted graffiti was then removed by sandblasting or particle blasting using a compressor and standard Arnold gun. This method may also be used to remove old paint which does not respond to paint stripper.

Highlighting engravings for public display

The top few millimetres of rock surfaces invariably differ in colour from the parent rock below. In most cases, this colour change is due to the presence of surface micro-organic material combined with altered (usually oxidised) surface minerals. The presence of surface mineral accretions such as desert varnish (Rosenfeld 1985:27-32) may also bring about surface contrast. Therefore engravings which penetrate this surface layer will be easily visible by virtue of both colour contrast and surface relief. It is the lack of these two features that renders Sydney engravings almost invisible to a large proportion of the visiting public. Here shallow groove profiles combine with the uniform colour of dark organic material over the entire rock surface, both in and outside the groove.

One such engraving site is at Bulgandry, near Gosford, where a walkway was constructed and visitors were encouraged by way of brochures and signs. Problems resulted with some visitors using stones to scratch the motifs, in order to highlight the grooves. This defacement resulted in the loss of the original groove profile. In some cases the well-meaning vandals were being misled by other superimposed engravings and unintentionally altered the motif (Plate 26). It then became necessary for the National Parks and Wildlife Service to highlight the original engravings, in order to avoid further vandalism and to maintain the original motif. To my knowledge this is the only Australian site where highlighting has been implemented. The result, eighteen months later, with the original motif outline restored, is shown in Plate 27.

The figure was highlighted by cleaning the groove profile of organic material, revealing the lighter colour of the rock beneath. The method is described below and shown in Plate 28.

1. Fresh water is trickled over the rock surface. The water is partly absorbed by the organic material, making it softer and less well bonded to the rock surface.

2. The groove is then lightly brushed using nylon brushes (described in Appendix 1). With the water still trickling over the surface, the organic material is easily removed.

As the site is exposed to rain, fresh water is unlikely to cause any adverse impact to the site. The main precaution taken when using this technique is not to brush outside the groove, which may be difficult to see before cleaning.

One concern with the technique is that it will need to be repeated approximately every twelve to eighteen months if visual contrast is to be maintained. There are presently no tested chemical treatments which may be applied to the rock surface to overcome this problem. Secondly, differential weathering in and outside the groove may result. As discussed in Chapter 8, this is difficult to monitor and it may be several years before it becomes apparent.

An alternative to cleaning the groove is to lighten the colour of the surrounding rock surface by wet-brushing the rock surface (using 100mm bristle brushes), and leaving the darker organic material contained inside the groove profile. This same effect is observable at West Head, north of Sydney, New South Wales, where large numbers of visitors have maintained a cleaner rock surface outside the groove by walking over the rock platform. Plans which are underway to construct viewing barriers and direct visitors off the site are likely to result in the motifs becoming difficult to see, in which case it may be desirable to wash the site as outlined above.

Other alternatives such as colouring the grooves using ochre or black pigments such as carbon black or manganese dioxide (black oxide) have been considered by site managers but not implemented.

An additional consideration of highlighting in this way is that the site manager's interpretation of what is engraving and what is not determines the final result. Once an engraved site is highlighted it becomes virtually impossible to see non-highlighted marks.

Side-lighting at night is a low impact method of enhancement. It is a non-erosive technique which does not require alteration of the imagery. Practical considerations such as cost and the limitations of evening viewing have, to date, precluded the implementation of this option.

8. SPECIALISED TECHNIQUES

Conserving paintings

Article 23 of the Burra Charter (1981) under the heading 'Conservation Practice' requires that 'Work on a place must be preceded by professionally prepared studies of the physical, documentary and other evidence, and the existing fabric recorded before any disturbance of the place'. In the cases of petroglyphs and pictographs, studies of the 'fabric' would include pigment identification.

Pigment identification

The use of sample analytical techniques for pigments is a specialised area requiring high technology laboratory equipment. Methods most frequently employed for this purpose include the scanning electron microscope with energy dispersive X-ray analysis, X-ray diffraction, infra-red spectroscopy, and other chemical and spot tests. Details of each of these techniques are given in Appendix 2 in the form of an extract from a report prepared by a consulting company for a study in Kakadu National Park. These techniques will also identify salts introduced to the pigments; such salts are considered to play a large part in the deterioration process (North 1987).

Pigment identification is expensive and requires small (pinhead size) samples to be taken from a site. It should only be carried out with a particular purpose in mind. For example, the pigment identification in the Kakadu study (North 1987) was preliminary to later testing of various products for consolidation and surface treatment. In an earlier study, Clarke (1976) identified two pigments in Western Australian sites, a red ochre (haematite, Fe_20_3) and a white pigment (Huntite, $MgCa(CO_30_4)$. Clarke (1977:91) later used this study for a pigment consolidation experiment. In New South Wales, clay-based pigments were identified using X-ray diffraction (Slanski 1979) for a pigment deterioration monitoring experiment (Lambert 1979).

Monitoring paintings for pigment loss

The monitoring of paintings for pigment loss is necessary for understanding the rate of site deterioration. This may allow the site manager to (a) observe the effectiveness of past conservation work; (b) justify the urgency of new or further conservation work; (c) justify more drastic proposals such as the introduction of surface consolidants; (d) correlate deterioration with other events such as bushfires, climatic events or salt accumulation where these are also being monitored.

Quantitative monitoring of pigment loss by relevant authorities is almost nonexistent in Australia and there are no publications which directly address this topic.

It is apparent that at sites where several coloured pigments are present, red ochre is exceedingly more durable than white and clay-based pigments. There are numerous examples where paintings appear to have been made in two colours, with only the red now remaining. Examples seen in the Kimberley in Western Australia (Clarke 1977:55), at Kakadu National Park, and at Flinders Island in northern Queensland demonstrate this phenomenon. Accordingly, it is considered that photographic monitoring is usually most appropriate for the more rapidly deteriorating white and clay-based pigments.

Photographic monitoring is being carried out at a site near Gosford, New South Wales. Here part of a hand-stencil executed in an orange, clay-based pigment is shown in Plates 29 and 30. It is clear from these plates that the process of flaking is the key to pigment loss and that quantitative estimates regarding the rate of loss can be established with time. This type of photographic monitoring is a specialised activity with these particular exposures being made by an experienced medical photographer, Pam Bagatella. The equipment used included a 'Nikon F2' body with 'Nikon' 104mm macro lens and a 'Sunpak Softlite 2000 M' flash.

Another example of appropriate photographic monitoring is at Flinders Island, in northern Queensland, where paintings are executed in red ochre and partially overpainted using a white clay-based pigment. It is apparent that more recent (post-contact) images retain most but not all of the original white overpainting while older figures retain varying amounts of this material. Such stark contrast between the red and white pigments, together with the implied rapid rate of white pigment loss, suggest that examples similar to those shown in Plates 31 and 32 would serve to monitor adequately the rate of white pigment loss. If indeed the rate is as rapid as implied by these observations then information gained from this procedure might serve to justify the use of consolidants in an attempt to preserve examples of complete bichrome paintings.

Using consolidants

Various consolidant types are discussed by Rosenfeld (1985:59-64) and they are not dealt with in detail here. The use of consolidants has generally been avoided by most state authorities. This is partly because there are many products on the market, all of which are advocated by their manufacturers but few of which have proved satisfactory when tested. There are, however, several products which are recommended by overseas and Australian conservators (eg, Schwartzbaum 1985:67-68; Clarke 1978:91-92) and the option of their use should not be overlooked by the site manager. If it can be demonstrated that rapid deterioration is taking place and that no alternative measures can be implemented to slow down the deterioration process, then the use of consolidants is considered a viable alternative. It is recommended that a cautious approach to the use of consolidants be adopted. They should initially be used on a trial basis, before applying them directly onto painted surfaces, or on a large scale. The selection of trial products and methods of application will vary depending on such factors as site type, rock type and presence of salts. It is strongly recommended that the use of consolidants be carried out by someone with past experience in site conservation.

Conserving engravings

Engraving sites occurring in arid areas are most often in a stable condition and require no conservation intervention. In fact there are probably more cases where well-meaning conservation has resulted in damage to such sites. One example where intervention was considered warranted is at Mootwingee in western New South Wales. Here tourists have removed various sections of engraved cap rock on a large engraved slope. This has caused adjoining engraved sections to loosen (Plate 33). A trial method employed with some success was to fill the created voids (where cap rock had been stolen) with a mix of sand and lime (in the ratio of 3 to 1), coloured to match the original rock. As can be seen from Plate 34, an exact colour match is difficult to obtain.

Weathering of engravings and rock durability

The rate of weathering of engravings will depend firstly on the durability of the rock surface, and secondly on the degree of exposure to weathering agents. Durability of the rock surface will be determined by the 'weatherability' of the minerals that constitute the rock surface. Monomineral rocks will generally be more resistant than polymineral rocks; for example, sandstones with a siliceous cement will be more durable than sandstones with clay or carbonate mineral cements. The porosity of the rock will also determine its durability. A porous rock is formed from solid minerals which are arranged in a structure with empty spaces called pores. Rocks with a high porosity will present a greater surface area on which weathering agents can act and will have considerable space for water, which is one of the most harmful agents in stone weathering. If the pores are interconnected the rock will have a high moisture content when saturated.

In most areas of Australia, engravings have been executed either on durable stone (Mootwingee, New South Wales; Chambers Gorge and Sacred Canyon, South Australia; Woodstock, Western Australia) or in shelters where more friable stone is protected from weathering agents (eg, Carnarvon Gorge, Queensland). Accordingly, most state authorities give low priority to reducing and/or monitoring engraving erosion. There are, however, two notable exceptions to this general rule. The first is the Mount Cameron West site in Tasmania which has already been discussed. Sydney rock engravings are the second; here, a unique and large complex of engravings has been executed on a sandstone with relatively low durability. Most sites are exposed to weathering agents because they are situated on flat rock outcrops. There is considerable *prima facie* evidence that these engravings have deteriorated significantly since European settlement (200 years). Because of the large number and area of distribution of these sites (some 1,000 sites distributed over an area of approximately 5,000 square kilometres), a proven conservation strategy needs to be developed before a large-scale conservation program can be implemented.

The inference from the above information is that engravings executed on soft, friable rock can be conserved by doing one or more of the following:

1. Increasing the durability of the sandstone by introducing a cement into the rock fabric.
2. Reducing the porosity of the rock.
3. Sheltering the exposed rock surface.

This would suggest a strategy of experimenting with a rock consolidant, combined with surface water diversion and the construction of a roof shelter. However, if we cannot measure the rate of erosion then we cannot assess the effectiveness of such conservation measures, and the necessary expenditure of funds cannot be justified. Accordingly, erosion monitoring is considered a priority task in such situations.

Monitoring engraving erosion

Monitoring engraving erosion is proving to be a slow and difficult task to date. There is no sure method of accurately monitoring groove profile change or predicting the life of engravings currently in use. There is, however, one monitoring technique which has been ongoing for several years. It is described below, principally because it is the only quantitative technique in use and, although the results to date are not conclusive, it serves to demonstrate the complex and long-term nature of this task.

The Traversing Micro-Erosion Meter (TMEM): The TMEM is basically a simple piece of apparatus; however, its description in detail is rather long and tedious and a brief outline is sufficient here in order to make readers aware of the technique. The instrument in use is fully described by Smith (1978:44-53) and is shown in Plate 35. Briefly, there are three reference studs permanently emplaced and forming a triangle on the rock surface. The TMEM houses an engineer's dial gauge which can be calibrated to measure accurately the height of fixed points within the triangle. Using this method the same points can be remeasured at a later date, thus monitoring erosion at certain fixed points on the site where the reference studs have been inserted.

The instrument has been in use on Hawkesbury Sandstone at various Sydney engraving sites for eight years. The unpublished results remain inconclusive over this period, with erosion being difficult to measure due to the presence of mineral and organic accretions on the rock surface. Another shortcoming of the method is that it only measures absolute erosion of the rock surface over a scatter of fixed points and fails to monitor groove profile.

REFERENCES

Amoroso, G.G. and V. Fassina

1983 *Stone Decay and Conservation*, Elsevier, Amsterdam.

Bindon, P.

1976 *The Devil's Hands: A Survey of the Painted Shelters of the Shoalhaven River Basin*, unpublished BA Thesis, Australian National University, Canberra.

Bradstock, R.

1988 Research Officer (Botany), New South Wales National Parks and Wildlife Service, Sydney. Personal communication.

Clarke, J.

1976 Two Aboriginal Rock Art Pigments From Western Australia, Their Properties, Use and Durability, *Studies in Conservation* 21, 134-42.

1978 Conservation and Restoration of Painting and Engraving Sites in Western Australia. In C. Pearson (ed), *Conservation of Rock Art, Proceedings of the International Workshop on the Conservation of Rock Art, Perth, September 1977*, Institute for the Conservation of Cultural Material, Sydney, 89-94.

1978, 1988 Rock Art Conservator, Perth, Western Australia. Personal communications.

Clegg, J.

1984 Some Thoughts on the Interpretation of Prehistoric Pictures. In H. Sullivan (ed), *Visitors to Aboriginal Sites: Access, Control and Management, Proceedings of the 1983 Kakadu Workshop*, Australian National Parks and Wildlife Service, Canberra, 88-93.

Gale, F.

1984 The Protection of Aboriginal Rock Art From Tourists at Ubirr, Kakadu National Park. In H. Sullivan (ed), *Visitors to Aboriginal Sites: Access, Control and Management, Proceedings of the 1983 Kakadu Workshop*, Australian National Parks and Wildlife Service, Canberra, 32-40.

Gale, F. and J.M. Jacobs

1987 *Tourists and the National Estate: Procedures to Protect Australia's Heritage*, Australian Government Publishing Service, Canberra (Special Australian Heritage Publication Series 6).

Gillespie, D.A. (compiler)

1983 *The Rock Art Sites of Kakadu National Park: Some Preliminary Researc h Findings For Their Conservation and Management,* Australian National Parks and Wildlife Service, Canberra.

Haydock, P. and J. Rodda

1986 *A Survey of Rock Art Conservation in the Murchison/Wheat Belt Area of Western Australia: A Study of Past Treatments and New Methods of Measurements and Site Management,* unpublished report, Western Australian Heritage Committee and Western Australian Museum, Perth.

Heritage Council of New South Wales

1982 *Rising Damp and its Treatment,* Heritage Council of New South Wales, Sydney (Technical Information Sheet 1).

Hughes, P.J.

1976 Inferred Rates of Weathering in Sandstone Shelters in Southern NSW: Some Implications For the Preservation of Rock Art. In C. Pearson and G. Pretty (eds), *Proceedings of the First National Seminar on the Conservation of Cultural Material, Perth, 1973,* Institute for the Conservation of Cultural Material, Perth, 51-54.

Hughes, P.J., A.L. Watchman and M.E. Sullivan

1981 Conservation of the Mount Cameron West Engraving Site, *Papers and Proceedings of the Royal Society of Tasmania* 115, 211-22.

Lambert, D.J.

1979 Natural Silica Formation Over Aboriginal Charcoal Drawings Near Gosford NSW, *Institute for the Conservation of Cultural Material Bulletin* 5, 45-48.

1980 The Influence of Groundwater Salts in the Formation of Sandstone Shelters Near Gosford, NSW, *Institute for the Conservation of Cultural Material Bulletin* 6, 29-34.

Lewin, S.Z.

1982 The Mechanism of Masonry Decay Through Crystallisation. In N.S. Baer (ed), *Conservation of Historic Stone Buildings and Monuments,* National Academy Press, New York, 120-44.

Luckman, L.E.

1951 *Some Notes on the Excavation of Aboriginal Carvings at Mt Cameron West, Tasmania,* unpublished report to the Royal Society of Tasmania.

Naumann, I.D.

1983 The Biology of Mud Nesting Hymenoptera (and Their Associates) and Isoptera in Rock Shelters in the Kakadu Region, NT. In D.A. Gillespie (compiler), *The Rock Art Sites of Kakadu National Park, Some Preliminary Researc h Findings For Their Conservation and Management*, Australian National Parks and Wildlife Service, Canberra, 127-89.

North, N. and J. Clarke

1987 *Conservation of Post-estuarine Period Rock Art in Kakadu National Park*, unpublished report to Australian National Parks and Wildlife Service by Corlab.

Ollier, C.D.

1976 *Weathering*, Longman, London.

Pearson, C. (ed)

1978 *Conservation of Rock Art, Proceedings of the International Workshop on the Conservation of Rock Art, Perth, September 1977*, Institute for the Conservation of Cultural Material, Sydney.

Rosenfeld, A.

1985 *Rock Art Conservation in Australia*, Australian Government Publishing Service, Canberra (Special Australian Heritage Publication Series 2). Reprinted 1988.

1987 Senior Lecturer, Department of Prehistory and Anthropology, Faculty of Arts, The Australian National University, Canberra. Personal communication.

Rosenfeld, A. and J. Winston-Gregson

1983 Excavations at Nursery Swamp 2, Gudgenby Nature Reserve, Australian Capital Territory, *Australian Archaeology* 17, 48-58.

Schwartzbaum, P.M.

1985 The Role of Conservation Techniques in Rock Art Preservation, *Rock Art Research* 1, 65-70.

Slanski, E.

1979 *Mineral Identification*, Department of Mineral Resources, New South Wales, unpublished report to New South Wales National Parks and Wildlife Service.

Slater, P.

1970 *A Field Guide to Australian Birds* (Volume 2), Rigby, Sydney.

Smith, D.I.

1978 The Micro-erosion Meter: Its Application to the Weathering of Rock Surfaces. In C. Pearson (ed), *Conservation of Rock Art, Proceedings of the International Workshop on the Conservation of Rock Art, Perth, September 1977,* Institute for the Conservation of Cultural Material, 44-53.

Sullivan, H. (ed)

1984 *Visitors to Aboriginal Sites: Access, Control and Management, Proceedings of the 1983 Kakadu Workshop,* Australian National Parks and Wildlife Service, Canberra.

Sullivan, K.M.

1984 Monitoring Visitor Use and Visitor Management at Three Art Sites. In H. Sullivan (ed), *Visitors to Aboriginal Sites: Access, Control and Management, Proceedings of the 1983 Kakadu Workshop,* Australian National Parks and Wildlife Service, Canberra, 43-53.

Sullivan, S.M.

1985 Aboriginal Site Interpretation—Some Considerations, *ACT Heritage Seminars* 3, 11-23.

Wainwright, I.N.M.

1985 The State of Research in Rock Art: Rock Art Conservation Research in Canada, *Bolletino del Centro Camuno di Studi Preistorici* 22, 15-46.

Walsh, G.L.

1984a Archaeological Site Management in Carnarvon National Park. A Case History in the Dilemma of Presentation or Preservation. In H. Sullivan (ed), *Visitors to Aboriginal Sites: Access, Control and Management, Proceedings of the 1983 Kakadu Workshop,* Australian National Parks and Wildlife Service, Canberra, 1-14.

1984b *Managing the Archaeological Sites of the Sandstone Belt,* Central Queensland Aboriginal Corporation for Cultural Activities and Queensland National Parks and Wildlife Service, Brisbane.

1984c *Archaeological Significance of Flinders Island/Princess Charlotte Bay,* Queensland National Parks and Wildlife Service, Brisbane.

Ward, G.K. and S.M. Sullivan

1989 The Australian Institute of Aboriginal Studies' Rock Art Protection Program, *Rock Art Research* 6(1), 54-62.

Watson, J.A. and J.M. Flood

1987 Termite and Wasp Damage to Australian Rock Art, *Rock Art Research* 4, 17-28.

Webb, I.

1986 Senior Ranger, New South Wales National Parks and Wildlife Service, Gosford. Personal communications.

Winkler, E.M.

1973 *Stone: Properties, Durability in Man's Environment*, Springer Verlay, New York.

APPENDIX 1
SOME MATERIALS USED IN CONSERVATION

Item	Suppliers	Approx. Cost
Jewellers' hand-piece: 'Core-less Micromotor' hand-piece with LED speed indicator.	House of Jewellery 89 York St, Sydney (02 296663)	$800
Brushes to suit hand-piece available in nylon or steel. Recommended black nylon discs (20 x 3 mm).	as above	7 cents each
Generator: 'Dunlite 1000' 1,000 watts; 4.2 amps, frequency 50 Hz; Briggs and Stratton petrol-driven motor.	Phillips	
'Lissapol N' non-ionic detergent (20 litre drums only).	Available industrial detergent suppliers; alternatively, ask for non-ionic/non-caustic detergent.	
Long-fibre tissue paper (sheets each 970 x 1880 mm; minimum order 10 sheets).	Tokyo KYUKYODO 7-4, Ginza 5 chome Chuoo-ku, Tokyo JAPAN.	20,500 yen per 10 sheets

APPENDIX 2
SAMPLE ANALYTICAL TECHNIQUES

This section deals with analytical techniques most commonly used to identify pigments and their contaminants such as salts and mineral covers. Some of the techniques will also give information regarding the structure of the pigment. This material is taken directly from a report prepared by Corlab (1987) for the Australian National Parks and Wildlife Service. Their permission to reproduce this material is gratefully acknowledged.

Scanning electron microscope (SEM) with energy dispersive X-ray analysis (EDXA)

The SEM, like an optical microscope, gives an enlarged image of the sample being studied. The SEM used in this work provides a magnification of up to 30,000 times with resolution of individual particles down to 0.1 micron, although full power is very rarely required and most examination was done at magnifications of less than 1,000 times. The SEM used in this study was a low pressure type which did not require any pretreatment of the sample prior to examination.

The SEM operates by focusing a very small beam of electrons onto the sample and then collecting the back-scattered electrons. By moving the beam over the sample surface a picture is built up in much the same manner as with TV images. The intensity of the back-scattered electron beam at each point on the sample surface depends primarily on the atomic weight of the atoms at that point; hence minerals with high atomic weights appear bright and those of low atomic weight are dull. The resultant images are often strikingly different in contrast to the corresponding optical images.

When the electron beam strikes the sample surface some of the electrons interact with the sample atoms to produce X-rays. By collecting these X-rays and measuring their frequency and intensity an indication can be obtained of the sample composition (atoms of differing atomic number produce X-rays of different frequency). The X-rays from the sample are collected over a period of approximately thirty seconds and if during this period the beam scans over the entire sample, a general analysis is obtained. However optionally the beam can be immobilized at one point on the sample and this will give a point analysis. By locating the analysis point using the magnified SEM image, an analysis can be obtained of individual crystals or paint/pigment layers. As the electron beam does not penetrate far below the material surface the analysis obtained is essentially a surface analysis. If the surface being scanned is a natural surface, such as the outer surface of a painting, then the results obtained will show a large contribution due to surface salts and dust, and may not be representative of the bulk pigment. A better representation of the bulk pigment is obtained by either powdering the sample or by measuring at the edge fracture.

An important limitation of the EDXA facility is that low atomic weight elements do not give a detectable X-ray signal, and as a consequence elements with an atomic number of less than 24 are not detected. In practical terms this means that the following common elements cannot be detected by EDXA even when they are present in the sample in large amounts:

CATIONS:	Sodium, Lithium and Ammonium
ANIONS:	Carbonate, Oxides, Hydroxides, Nitrates, Oxilates and Organic Acid Salts
COMPOUNDS:	All organic compounds containing only Carbon, Hydrogen, Nitrogen or Oxygen

X-ray diffraction (XRD)

In XRD a fine beam of X-rays [is] fired into a powdered sample. As the X-rays pass through the sample they are deflected by the crystal planes. The deflected X-rays are collected and the angles of deflection and the intensity of the beams at each angle of deflection are recorded. Both the intensity and angle of deflection are related to the shape of the crystal structures present in the sample and to the types of atoms in the sample.

Sample identification is normally performed by comparing the observed X-ray diffraction pattern with the known patterns of previously studied minerals. To assist this process tables are available which list the X-ray diffraction patterns for known minerals.

The main limitation with XRD is that the unknown sample may contain mineral types which have not previously been recorded. This is quite common with rock art pigments as there has been comparatively little previous study done on rock surface mineralogy. In addition, if a sample contains several different mineral types then the resultant XRD pattern can be exceedingly complex. Some minerals, such as quartz, have a very intense X-ray pattern and they will generally show strongly even when they are present in relatively small amounts. By contrast amorphous substances have very weak patterns and can readily avoid detection.

Infra-red spectroscopy (IR)

In infra-red spectroscopy a beam of light with a narrow frequency range is passed through a prepared specimen and the amount of light absorbed by that specimen is recorded. The frequency of the light beam is slowly changed from 2.5 to 50 microns and the absorption as a function of wavelength is continuously recorded. In this study all the samples were prepared by mechanically grinding to a fine powder and then incorporating this powder into a KBr [potassium bromide] disc.

In this region of the light spectrum all absorptions are due to covalent bonds within the sample molecules such as C-H, C-O, Si-O, H-O, Fe-O and similar bonds. Ionic bonds, such as in NaCl, do not absorb in this region of the spectrum. Consequently IR gives information only on the types of covalent bonds which exist in the sample. In compounds having a mixture of ionic and covalent bonds, such as calcium carbonate, only the covalent bonds (such as C-O) will show absorption peaks. However the position of these peaks can be influenced by the ionic bonds present in the compound. A consequence of this selective absorption is that compounds having the same covalent bonds, but different ionic bonds, will show very similar IR spectra.

With IR spectroscopy those groups having intense peaks can be readily identified even when present at quite low concentrations. In rock art pigments common compounds with these characteristics are oxilates [sic], carbonates, organic materials and clays. Other compounds which have either no IR peaks (such as KCl, NaCl) or only broad peaks (such as FeOOH) will not produce distinctive spectra and consequently may not be detected at all by this method.

Spot tests

Carbonates, oxilates [sic] and clays are three common minerals found in white pigments. These three minerals react differently with dilute acid and this provides a quick spot test for identification purposes. By spotting multi-layered samples with dilute hydrochloric acid whilst the samples were under an optical microscope, it was possible to distinguish which compounds were present in which layer. This distinction used was:

Carbonates—React rapidly, dissolve and form copious gas bubbles;
Oxilates [sic]—React slowly with gradual gas formation;
Clays—No reaction but may disperse slowly; no dissolution.

(From North and Clarke 1978 Appendix 1. Reproduced with the permission of the authors and the Australian National Parks and Wildlife Service.)

APPENDIX 3: THE BURRA CHARTER

Preamble

Having regard to the International Charter for the Conservation and Restoration of Monuments and Sites (Venice 1966), and the Resolutions of 5th General Assembly of the International Council on Monuments and Sites (ICOMOS) (Moscow 1978), the following Charter was adopted by Australia ICOMOS on 19th August 1979 at Burra Burra. Revisions were adopted on 23rd February 1981 and on 23 April 1988.

Explanatory Notes

These notes do not form part of the Charter and may be added to by Australia ICOMOS.

Definitions

Article 1. For the purpose of this Charter:

1.1 *Place* means site, area, building or other work, group of buildings or other works together with associated contents and surroundings.

Article 1.1
Place includes structures, ruins, archaeological sites and landscapes modified by human activity.

1.2 *Cultural significance* means aesthetic, historic, scientific or social value for past, present or future generations.

1.3 *Fabric* means all the physical material of the *place.*

1.4 *Conservation* means all the processes of looking after a *place* so as to retain its *cultural significance.* It includes *maintenance* and may according to circumstance include *preservation*, *restoration*, *reconstruction* and *adaptation* and will be commonly a combination of more than one of these.

1.5 *Maintenance* means the continuous protective care of the *fabric*, contents and setting of a *place*, and is to be distinguished from repair. Repair involves *restoration* or *reconstruction* and it should be treated accordingly.

Article 1.5
The distinctions referred to in Article 1.5, for example in relation to roof gutters, are:

maintenance — regular inspection and cleaning of gutters

repair involving restoration — returning of dislodged gutters to their place

repair involving reconstruction — replacing decayed gutters.

1.6 *Preservation* means maintaining the *fabric* of a *place* in its existing state and retarding deterioration.

1.7 *Restoration* means returning the EXISTING *fabric* of a *place* to a known earlier state by removing accretions or by reassembling existing components without the introduction of new material.

1.8 *Reconstruction* means returning a *place* as nearly as possible to a known earlier state and is distinguished by the introduction of materials (new or old) into the *fabric.* This is not to be confused with either re-creation or conjectural reconstruction which are outside the scope of this Charter.

1.9 *Adaptation* means modifying a *place* to suit proposed compatible uses.

1.10 *Compatible use* means a use which involves no change to the culturally significant fabric, changes which are substantially reversible, or changes which require a minimal impact.

Conservation Principles

Article 2. The aim of *conservation* is to retain the *cultural significance* of a *place* and must include provision for its security, its *maintenance* and its future.

Article 2
Conservation should not be undertaken unless adequate resources are available to ensure that the fabric is not left in a vulnerable state and that the cultural significance of the place is not impaired. However, it must be emphasised that the best conservation often involves the least work and can be inexpensive.

Article 3. *Conservation* is based on a respect for the existing *fabric* and should involve the least possible physical intervention. It should not distort the evidence provided by the *fabric.*

Article 3
The traces of additions, alterations and earlier treatments on the fabric of a place are evidence of its history and uses.

Conservation action should tend to assist rather than to impede their interpretation.

Article 4. *Conservation* should make use of all the disciplines which can contribute to the study and safeguarding of a *place.* Techniques employed should be traditional but in some circumstances they may be modern ones for which a firm scientific basis exists and which have been supported by a body of experience.

Article 5. *Conservation* of a *place* should take into consideration all aspects of its *cultural significance* without unwarranted emphasis on any one aspect at the expense of others.

Article 6. The conservation policy appropriate to a *place* must first be determined by an understanding of its *cultural significance.*

Article 6
An understanding of the cultural significance of a place is essential to its proper conservation. This should be achieved by means of a thorough investigation resulting in a report embodying a statement of cultural significance. The formal adoption of a statement of cultural significance is an essential prerequisite to the preparation of a conservation policy.

Article 7. The conservation policy will determine which uses are compatible.

Article 7
Continuity of the use of a place in a particular way may be significant and therefore desirable.

Article 8. *Conservation* requires the maintenance of an appropriate visual setting: e.g., form, scale, colour, texture and materials. No new construction, demolition or modification which would adversely affect the setting should be allowed. Environmental instrusions which adversely affect appreciation or enjoyment of the *place* should be excluded.

Article 8
New construction work, including infill and additions, may be acceptable, provided:

it does not reduce or obscure the cultural significance of the place

it is in keeping with Article 8.

Article 9. A building or work should remain in its historical location. The moving of all or part of a building or work is unacceptable unless this is the sole means of ensuring its survival.

Article 9
Some structures were designed to be readily removable or already have a history of previous moves, e.g. prefabricated dwellings and poppet-heads. Provided such a structure does not have a strong association with its present site, its removal may be considered.

If any structure is moved, it should be moved to an appropriate setting and given an appropriate use. Such action should not be to the detriment of any place of cultural significance.

Article 10. The removal of contents which form part of the *cultural significance* of the *place* is unacceptable unless it is the sole means of ensuring their security and *preservation*. Such contents must be returned should changed circumstances make this practicable.

Conservation Processes

Preservation

Article 11. *Preservation* is appropriate where the existing state of the *fabric* itself constitutes evidence of specific *cultural significance*, or where insufficient evidence is available to allow other conservation processes to be carried out.

Article 11
Preservation protects fabric without obscuring the evidence of its construction and use.

The process should always be applied:

where the evidence of the fabric is of such significance that it must not be altered. This is an unusual case and likely to be appropriate for archaeological remains of national importance;

where insufficient investigation has been carried out to permit conservation policy decisions to be taken in accord with Articles 23 to 25.

New construction may be carried out in association with preservation when its purpose is the physical protection of the fabric and when it is consistent with Article 8.

Article 12. *Preservation* is limited to the protection, *maintenance* and, where necessary, the stabilization of the existing *fabric* but without the distortion of its *cultural significance.*

Article 12
Stabilization is a process which helps keep fabric intact and in a fixed position. When carried out as a part of preservation work it does not introduce new materials into the fabric. However, when necessary for the survival of the fabric, stabilization may be effected as part of a reconstruction process and new materials introduced. For example, grouting or the insertion of a reinforcing rod in a masonry wall.

Restoration

Article 13. *Restoration* is appropriate only if there is sufficient evidence of an earlier state of the *fabric* and only if returning the *fabric* to that state reveals the *cultural significance* of the *place.*

Article 13
See explanatory note for Article 2.

Article 14. *Restoration* should reveal anew culturally significant aspects of the *place.* It is based on respect for all the physical, documentary and other evidence and stops at the point where conjecture begins.

Article 15. *Restoration* is limited to the reassembling of displaced components or removal of accretions in accordance with Article 16.

Article 16. The contributions of all periods to the *place* must be respected. If a *place* includes the *fabric* of different periods, revealing the *fabric* of one period at the expense of another can only be justified when what is removed is of slight *cultural significance* and the *fabric* which is to be revealed is of much greater *cultural significance.*

Reconstruction

Article 17. *Reconstruction* is appropriate only where a *place* is incomplete through damage or alteration and where it is necessary for its survival, or where it reveals the *cultural significance* of the *place* as a whole.

Article 18. *Reconstruction* is limited to the completion of a depleted entity and should not constitute the majority of the *fabric* of a *place.*

Article 19. *Reconstruction* is limited to the reproduction of *fabric,* the form of which is known from physical and/or documentary evidence. It should be identifiable on close inspection as being new work.

Adaptation

Article 20. *Adaptation* is acceptable where the *conservation* of the *place* cannot otherwise be achieved, and where the *adaptation* does not substantially detract from its *cultural significance.*

Article 21. *Adaptation* must be limited to that which is essential to a use for the *place* determined in accordance with Articles 6 and 7.

Article 22. *Fabric* of *cultural significance* unavoidably removed in the process of *adaptation* must be kept safely to enable its future reinstatement.

Conservation Practice

Article 23. Work on a *place* must be preceded by professionally prepared studies of the physical, documentary and other evidence, and the existing *fabric* recorded before any intervention in the *place.*

Article 24. Study of a *place* by any intervention in the *fabric* or by archaeological excavation should be undertaken where necessary to provide data essential for decisions on the *conservation* of the *place* and/or to secure evidence about to be lost or made inaccessible through necessary *conservation* or other unavoidable action. Investigation of a *place* for any other reason which requires physical disturbance and which adds substantially to a scientific body of knowledge may be permitted, provided that it is consistent with the conservation policy for the *place.*

Article 25. A written statement of conservation policy must be professionally prepared setting out the *cultural significance* and proposed *conservation* procedure together with justification and supporting evidence, including photographs, drawings and all appropriate samples.

Article 25
The procedure will include the conservation processes referred to in Article 1.4 and other matters described in Guidelines to the Burra Charter: Conservation Policy.

Article 26. The organisation and individuals responsible for policy decisions must be named and specific responsibility taken for each such decision.

Article 27. Appropriate professional direction and supervision must be maintained at all stages of the work and a log kept of new evidence and additional decisions recorded as in Article 25 above.

Article 28. The records required by Articles 23, 25, 26 and 27 should be placed in a permanent archive and made publicly available.

Article 29. The items referred to in Articles 10 and 22 should be professionally catalogued and protected.

Words in italics are defined in Article 1.

INDEX

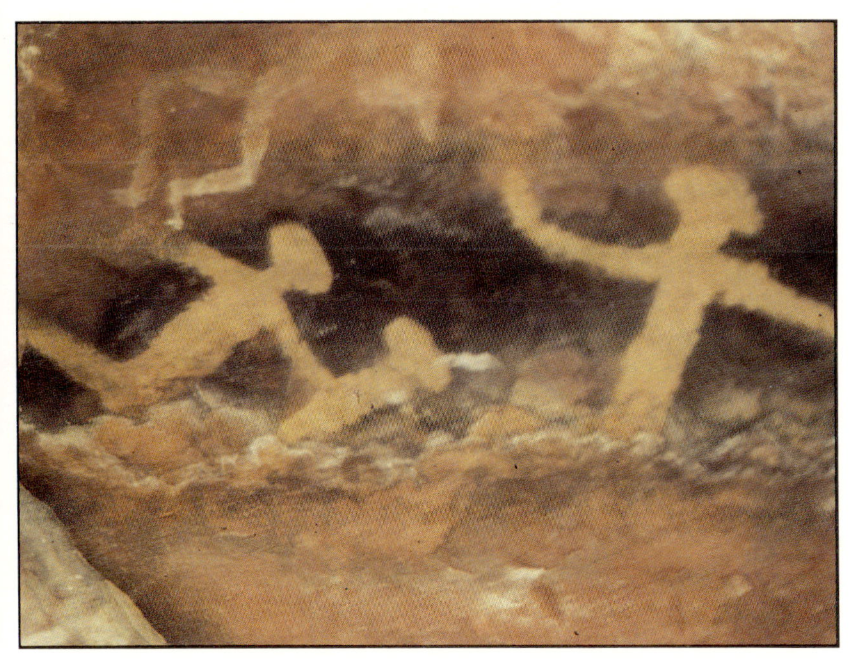

Plate 1.

Direct water erosion of paintings: This painted surface at Mount Grenfell, New South Wales shows motifs which have been sharply cut by water flowing across the rock face. Such figure-cutting indicates the need for the use of driplines.

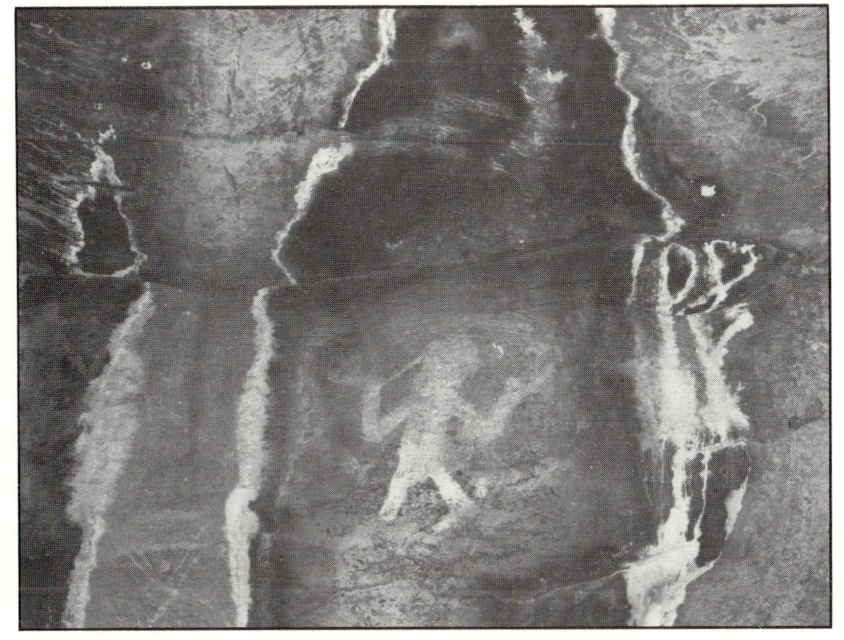

Plate 2.

Direct water erosion of paintings: This site exhibits evidence of surface water erosion. The clean rock zone at both sides of the photo is the area of water flow. The permanently dry area containing images is located in the black zone (centre), and is bordered by a white salt zone which is often the hydrated form of the black material. Application of a dripline would interrupt the surface water flow.

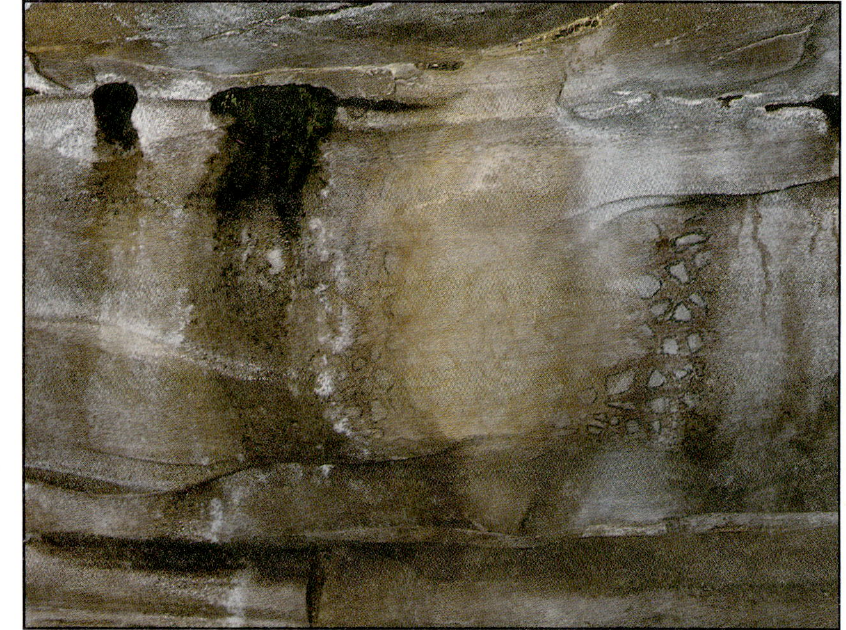

Plate 3.
Silica from solution forming over and preserving drawings: Silica mineralisation occurring over painted images at a site near Nowra, New South Wales. Note that the silica appears to be derived from water seeps located at each end of the photo. At the centre, mineralisation is less apparent and pigments are less well preserved.

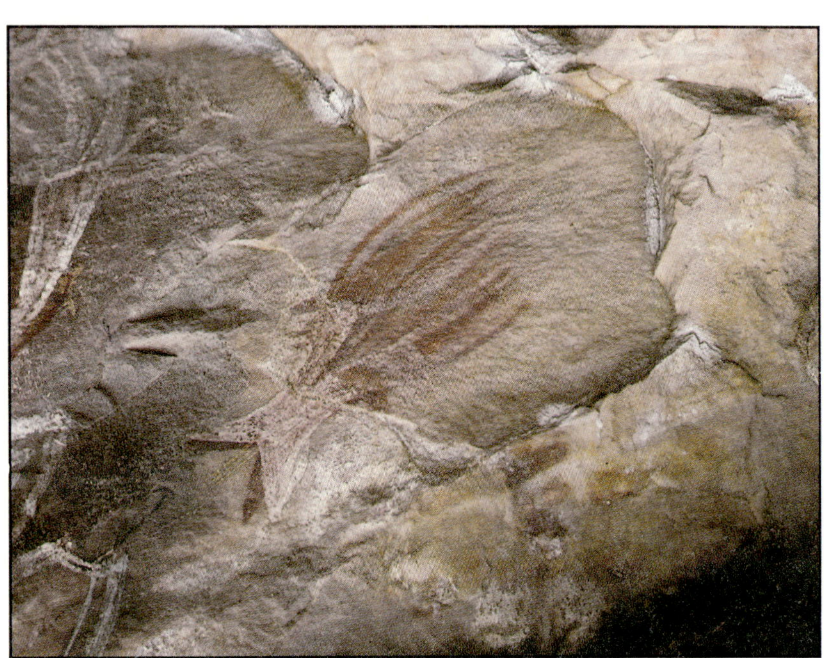

Plate 4.
Silica from solution forming over and preserving drawings: Silica mineralisation has preserved the rear part of this fish figure in Kakadu National Park, Northern Territory. Note that the silica is absent from the much deteriorated head section of the fish motif.

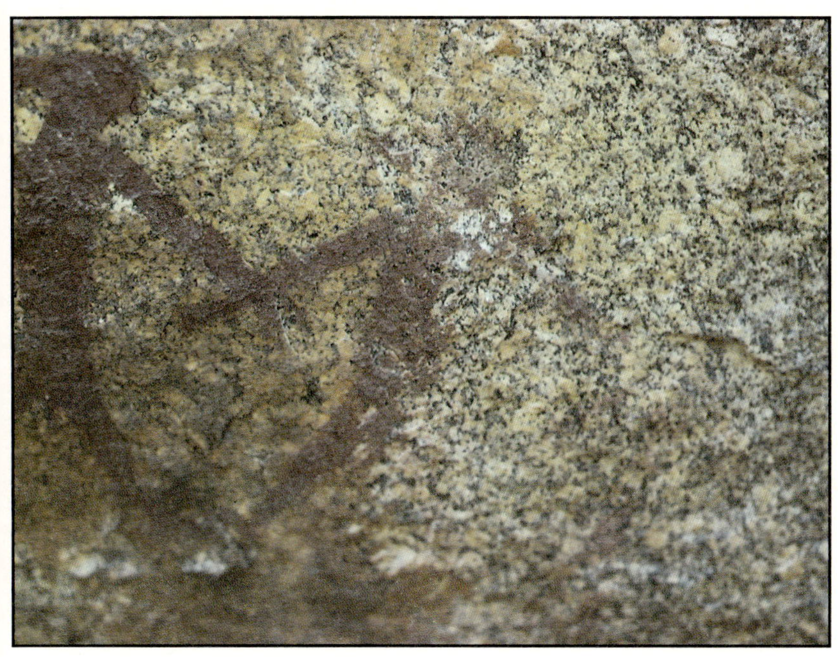

Plate 5.
Frost damage to a painting in a granite shelter: It is considered that the damage to this site is predominantly caused by frost. Freshly pitted rock occurs adjacent to undamaged motifs. There is no sharp vertical line cutting figures as displayed by surface water flow.

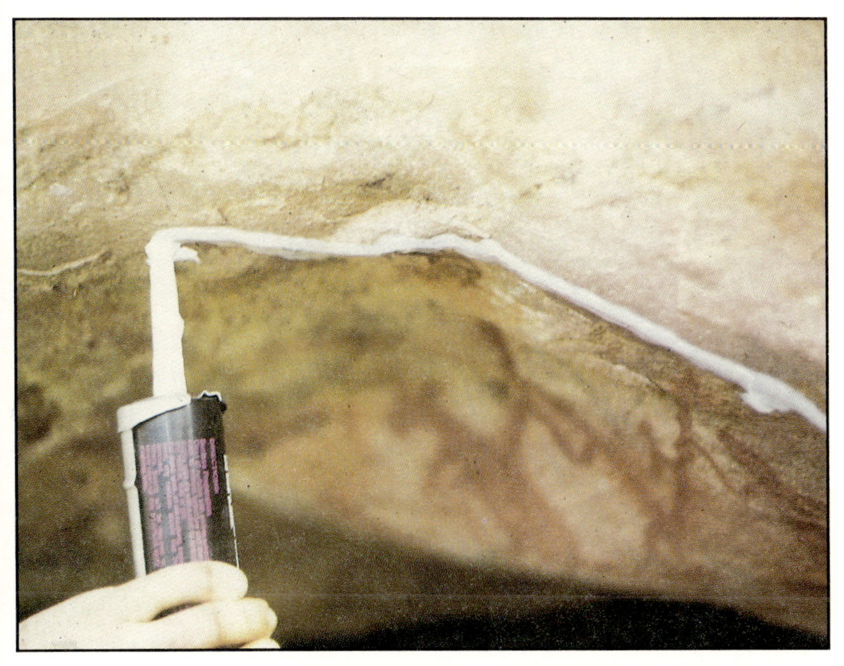

Plate 6.
Applying a silicone dripline: A silicone bead dripline being installed in a shelter near Cobar, New South Wales.

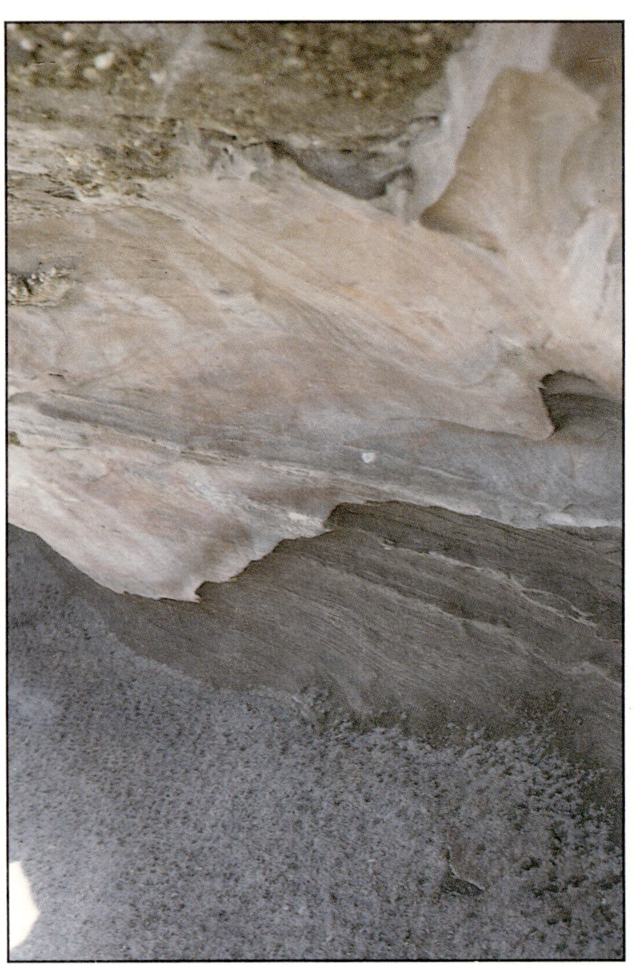

Plate 7.
Salt damage: Salt deterioration undercutting a painting site in North Queensland.

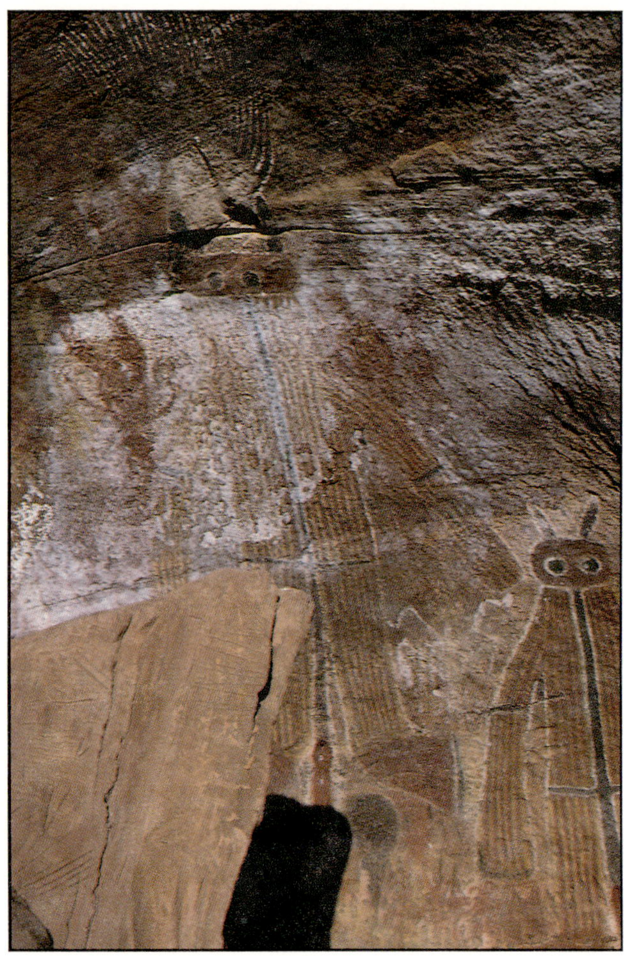

Plate 8.
Salt damage: Salts visible within a painted surface, Delemere, Northern Territory.

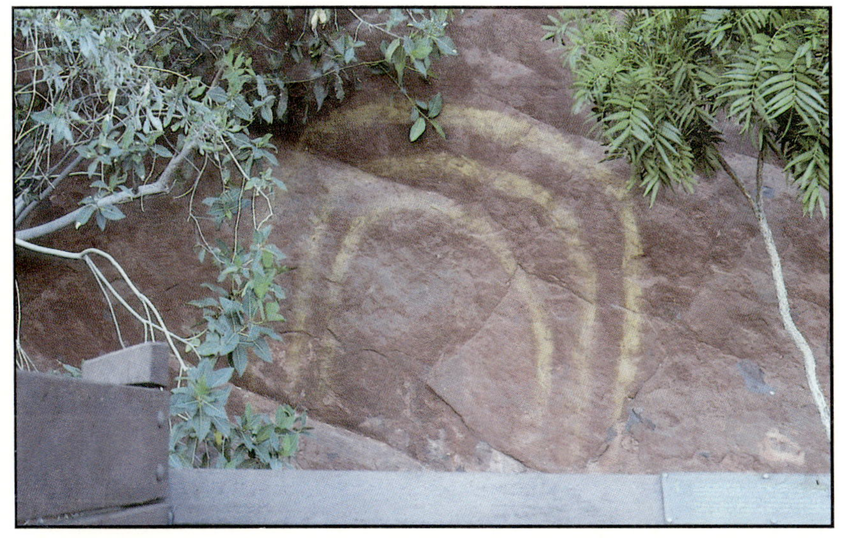

Plate 9.
Vegetation damage: An example of vegetation growing too close to a site (Lawn Hill, North Queensland). Direct rubbing of the rock surface would eventually damage the images at this site; vegetation had previously been removed from this site but had since regrown.

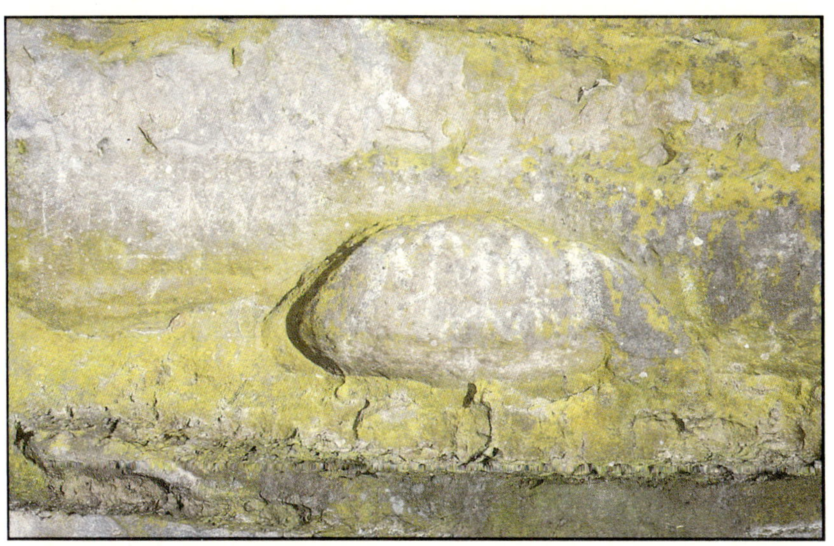

Plate 10.
Micro-organic growth over paintings before and after treatment: Proliferating microflora in a site known as Quiera, Morton National Park, New South Wales. Old photographs indicate that growth has significantly increased since the 1950s.

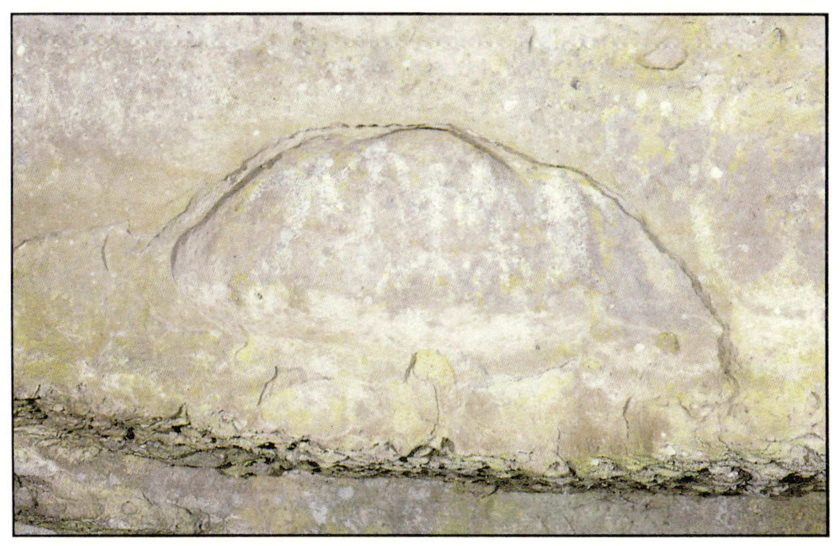

Plate 11.
Micro-organic growth over paintings before and after treatment: The Quiera site after cleaning. Note that complete removal of microflora has not been possible.

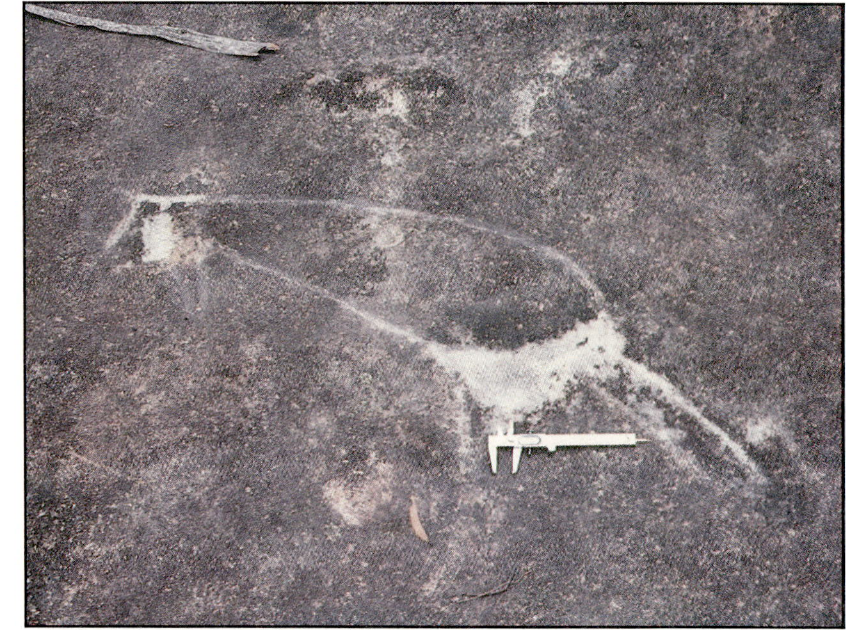

Plate 12.
Lichen damage to Sydney engravings: A site at Burragurra, near Gosford, New South Wales. The dead lichen leaves behind a soft, friable area of sandstone which is easily eroded.

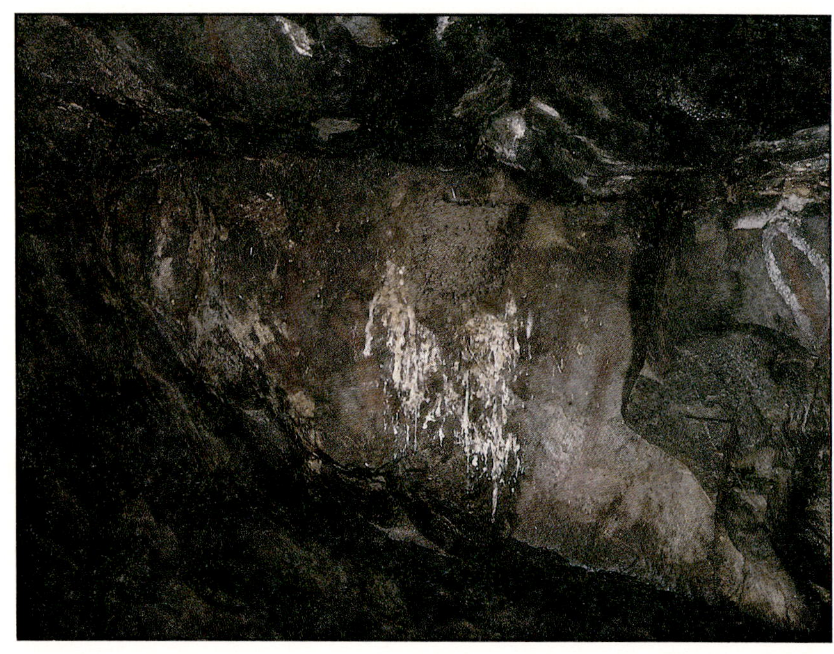

Plate 13.
Swallows nest damage to a painting site: Swallows nest and droppings at a site in the Adelaide Hills, South Australia.

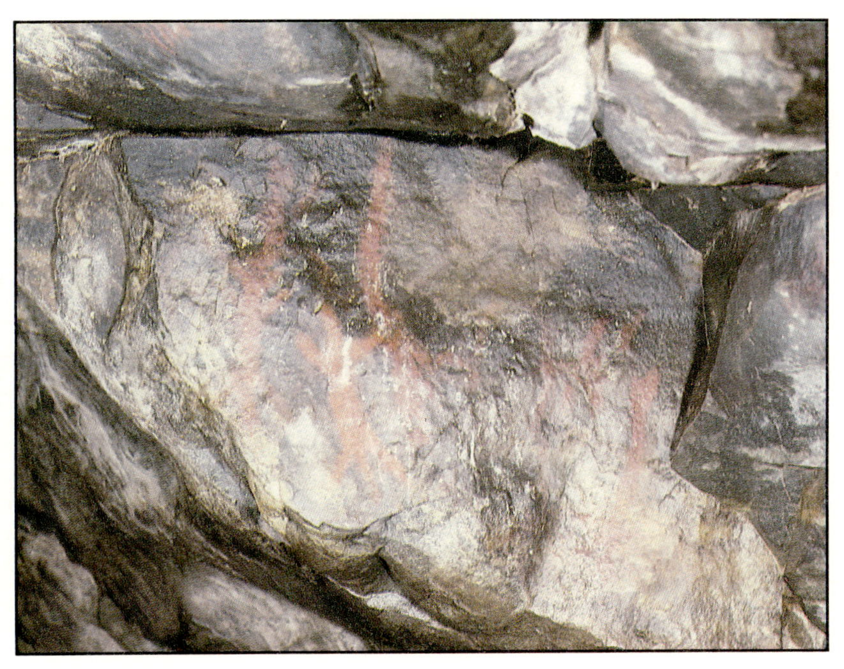

Plate 14.
Swallows nest damage to a painting site: The same site as Plate 13 after cleaning. Note the permanent removal of paintings beneath the former mud nest, and the incomplete removal of droppings to avoid excessive washing.

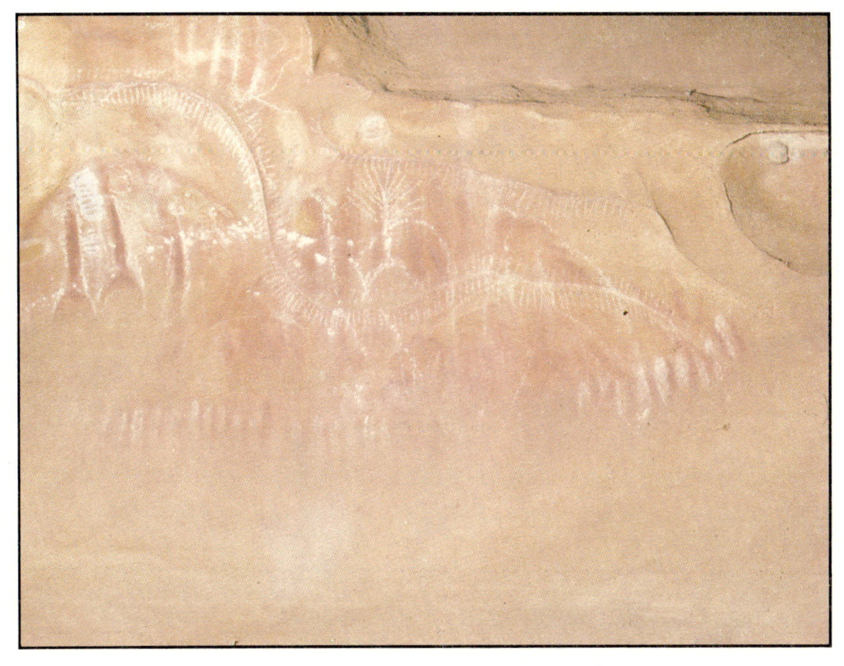

Plate 15.
Dust damage: Airborne material obscuring the lower half of paintings at Arkaroo Rock, South Australia. This material was firmly fixed to the rock surface and confined to the lower sections of the shelter. It could only partly be removed by washing the site using long-fibre tissue. More work will need to be carried out to determine the mechanism and nature of this problem, in particular the role of airborne salts.

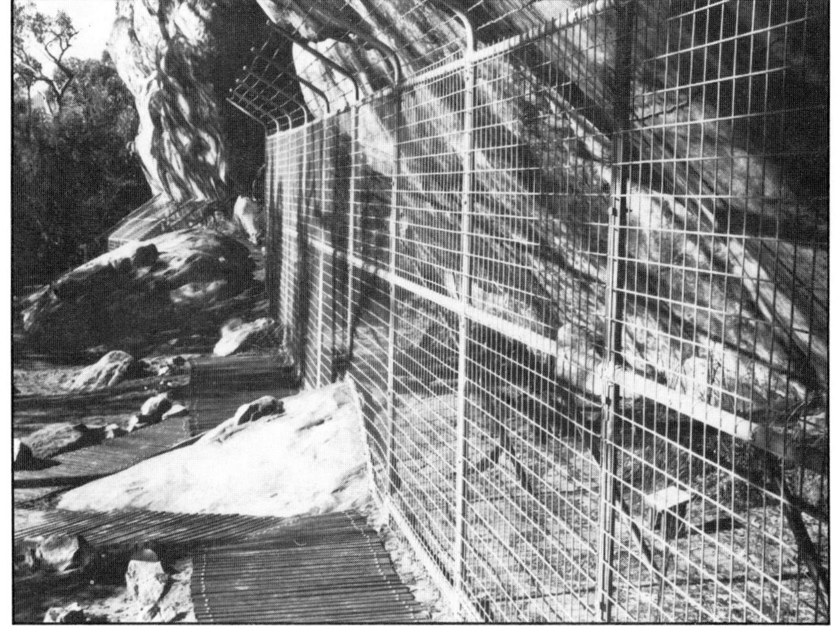

Plate 16.
Mesh screens and their visual impact: An example of a mesh screen in the Grampians district of Victoria. While the screens undoubtedly detract from the aesthetics of the site, few complaints are received from visitors.

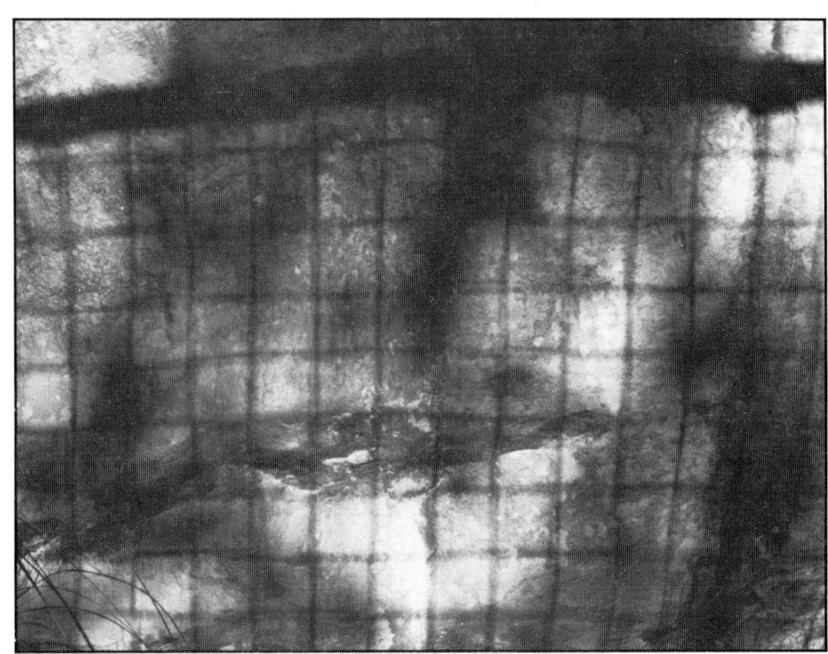

Plate 17.
Impact of a mesh screen on viewing pictographs: The shadow cast by the mesh screen makes the figure in this plate difficult to see or to photograph.

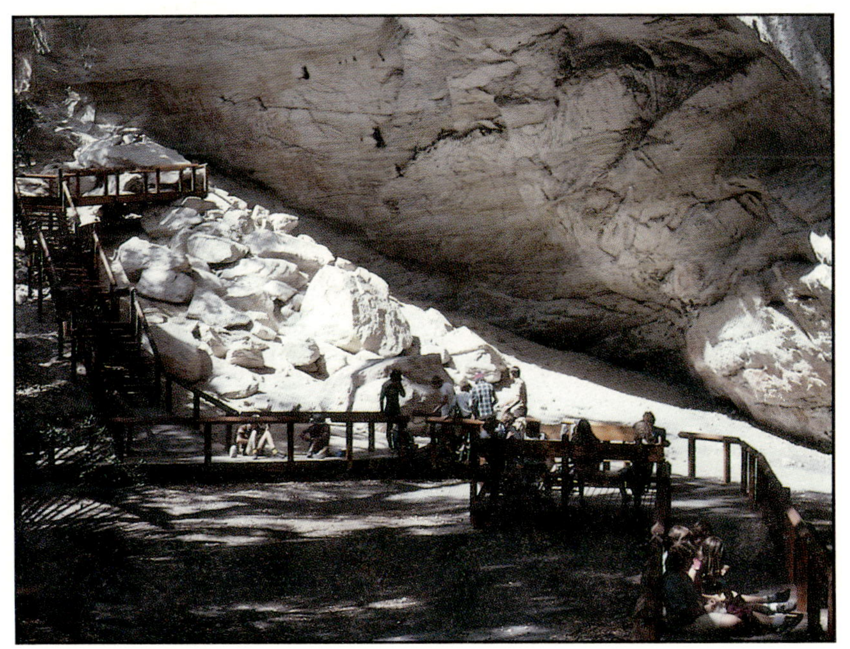

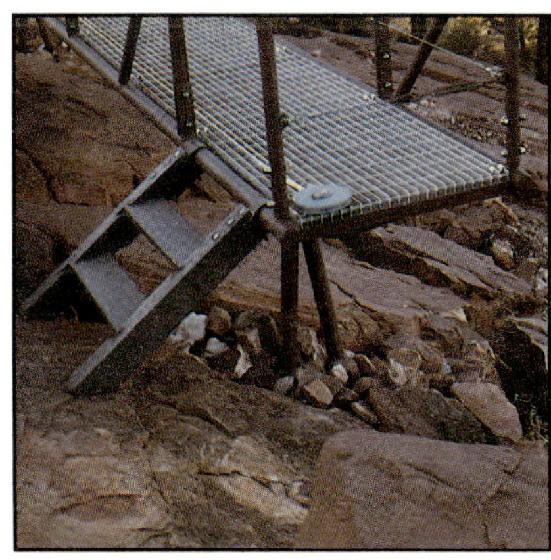

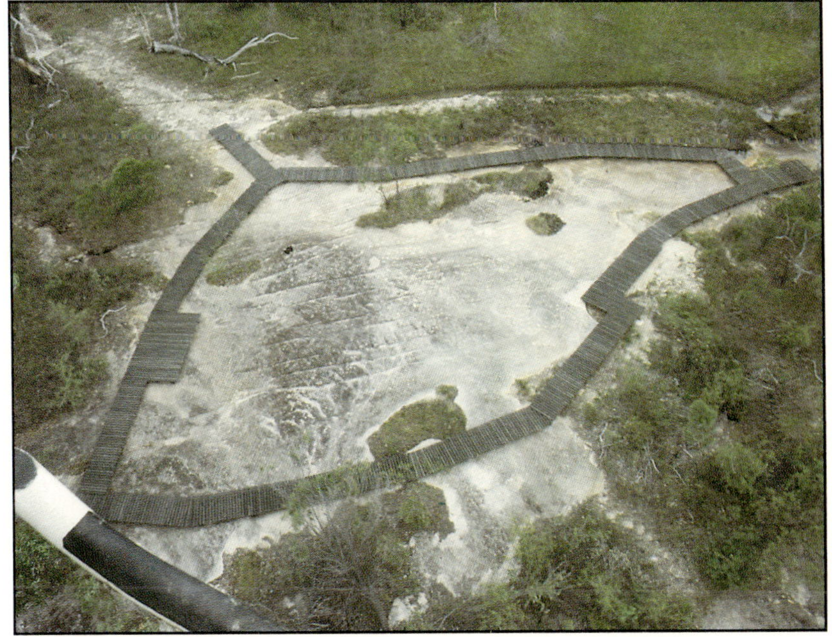

Plate 18.
Walkways: Walkway at Mootwingee, New South Wales. Built from metal, the walkway does not blend in well with the environment.

Plate 19.
Walkways: Built from local Cypress Pine, this walkway at Carnarvon Gorge in Queensland is suited to the site context.

Plate 20.
Walkways: An aerial view of a walkway on an engraving site at Bulgandry, near Gosford, New South Wales. Following a visitor survey, the design of the walkway was slightly modified.

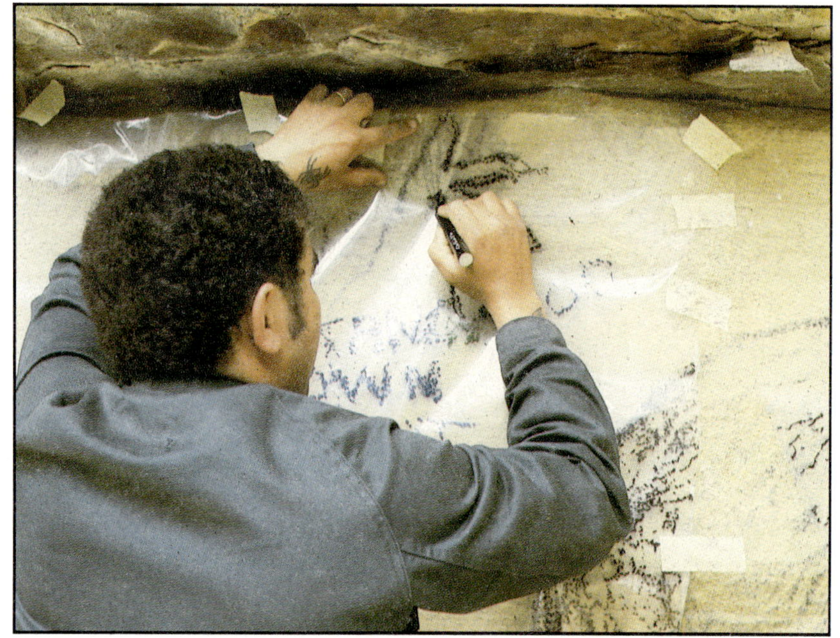

Plate 21.
Vandalism: Recording both the art and graffiti present before attempting to remove graffiti from a site near Wilton, New South Wales.

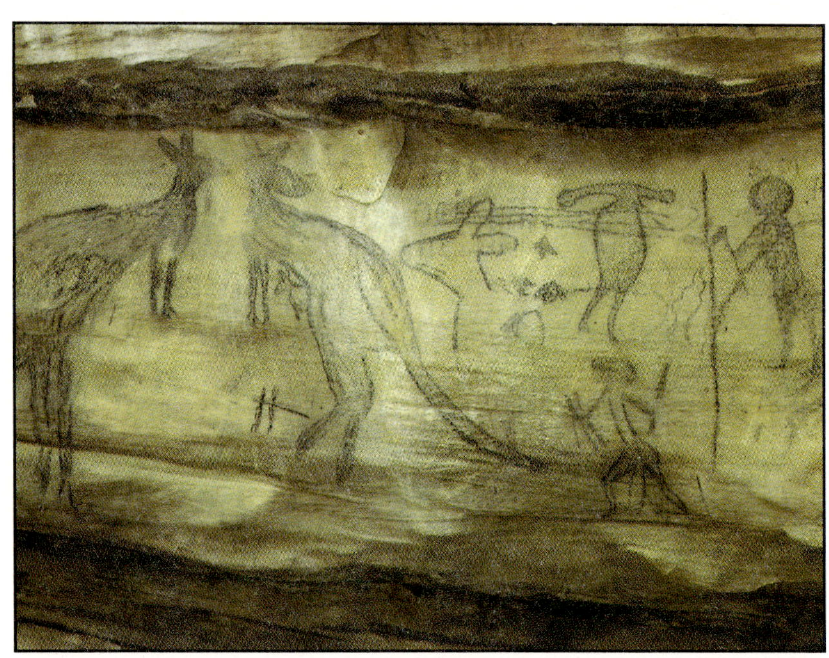

Plate 22.
Vandalism: An example of post-contact art at a site near Wilton, New South Wales. Graffiti in the form of names and initials has been removed from this site.

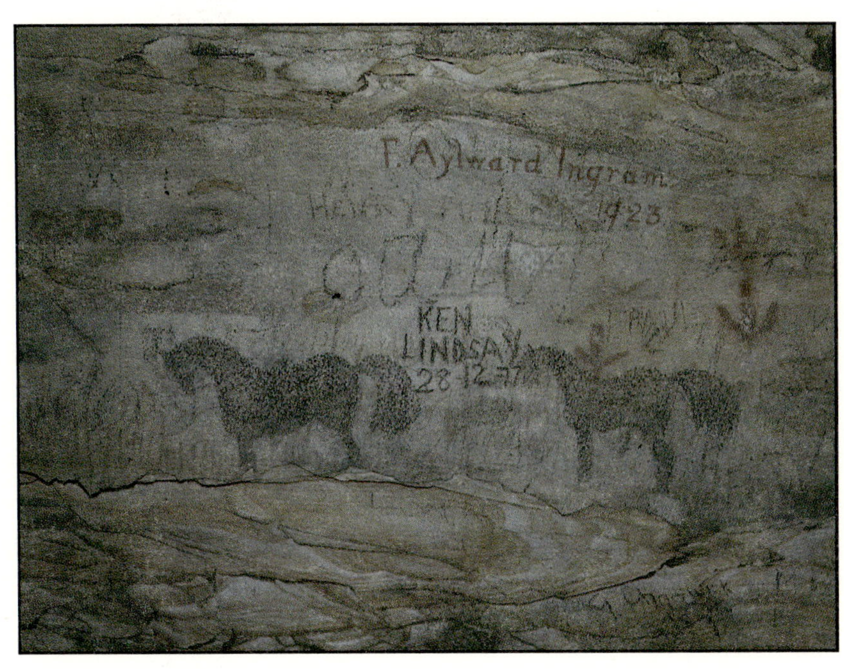

Plate 23.
Vandalism: A vandalised site at Nullo Mountain, in Wollemi National Park, New South Wales.

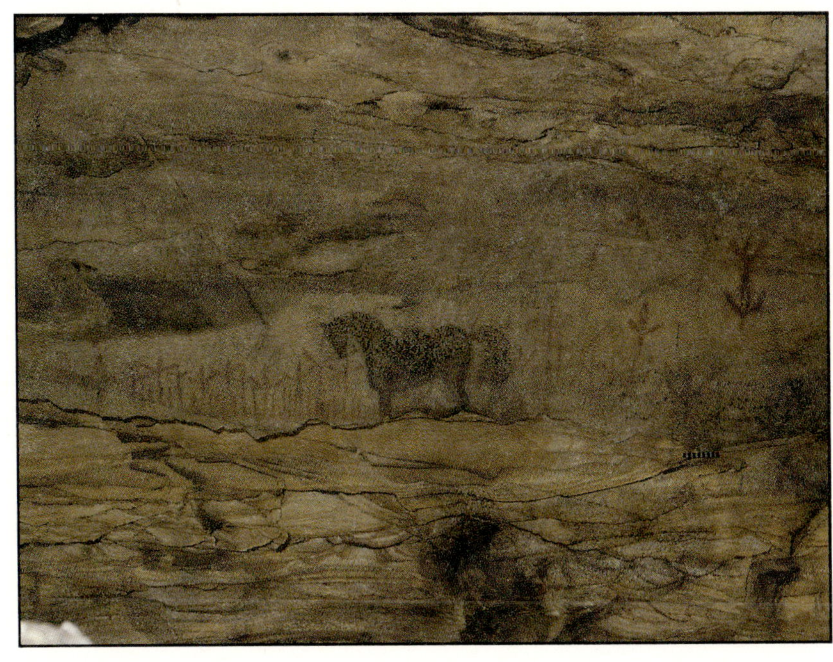

Plate 24.
Vandalism: The Nullo Mountain site after removal of graffiti. The horse which was left was reportedly drawn by a bushranger and the horse which was removed was identified as a later copy.

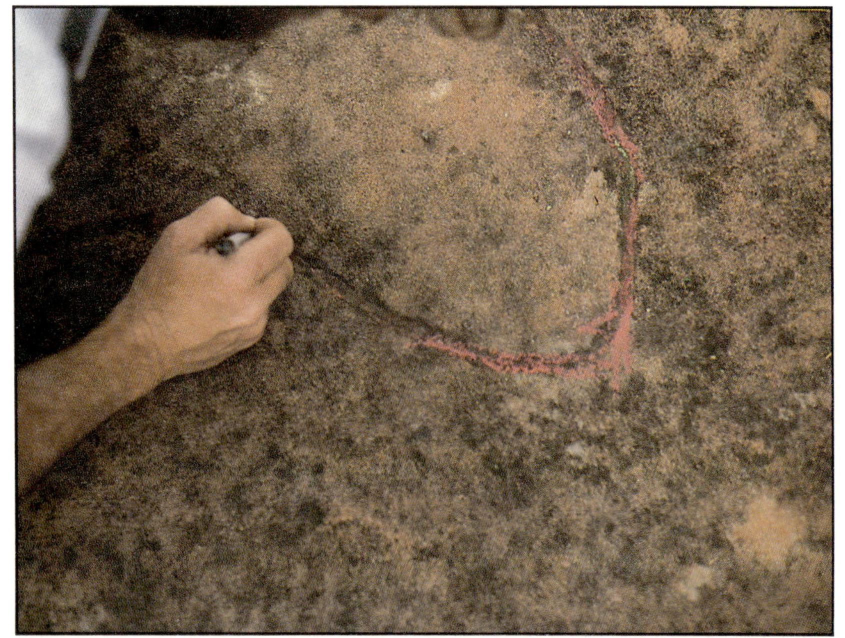

Plate 25.
Vandalism: Removing wax (waterproof) crayon from an engraving using a bronze brush at West Head in Kuring-gai Chase National Park, New South Wales.

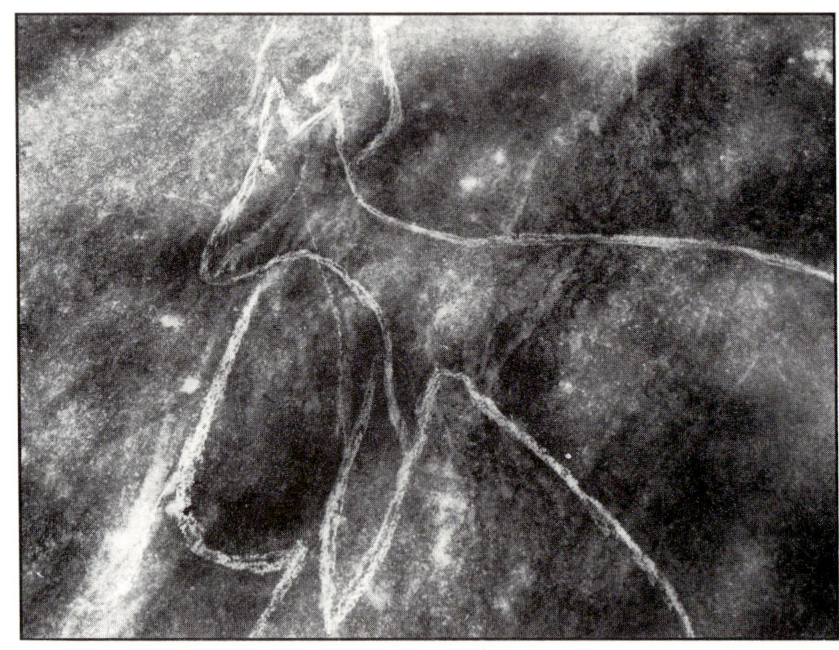

Plate 26.
Vandalism: An engraving at Bulgandry, New South Wales, which has been scratched-in by vandals, leading to alteration of motif design. The short original front paw is only just discernible in the photograph. The vandal has mistakenly extended the paw by following a superimposed engraving.

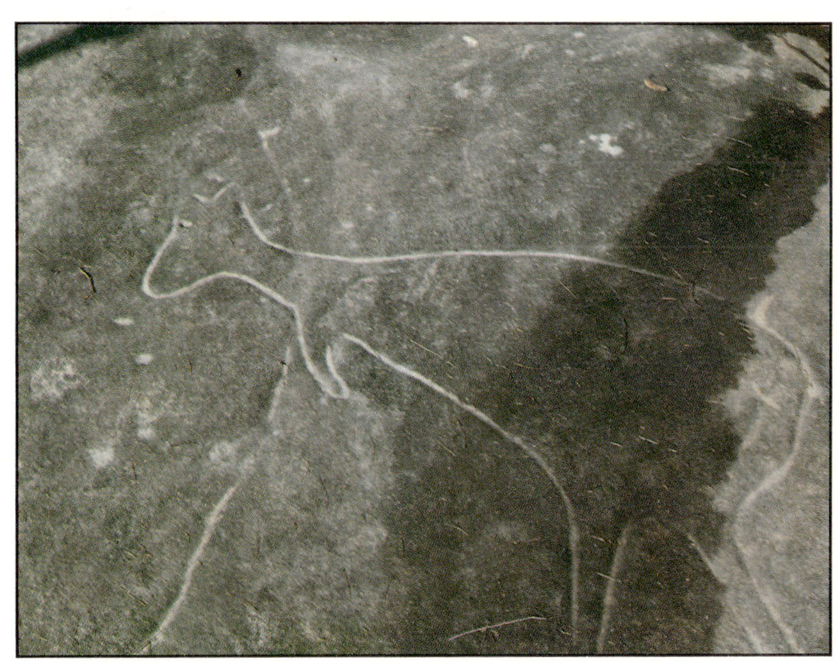

Plate 27.
Bulgandry, New South Wales: The restored engraving eighteen months after the first treatment.

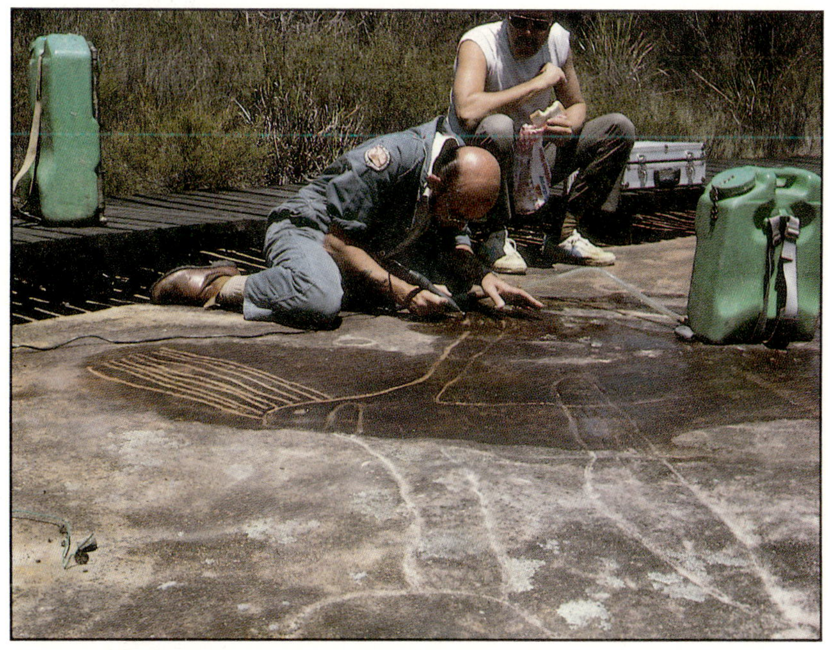

Plate 28.
Highlighting sandstone engravings: Groove cleaning to highlight engravings at Bulgandry, a developed site where figures were difficult to see and where vandalism was occurring. Highlighting is done by washing dark micro-organic material out of the groove using water and applying an electrically driven nylon brush.

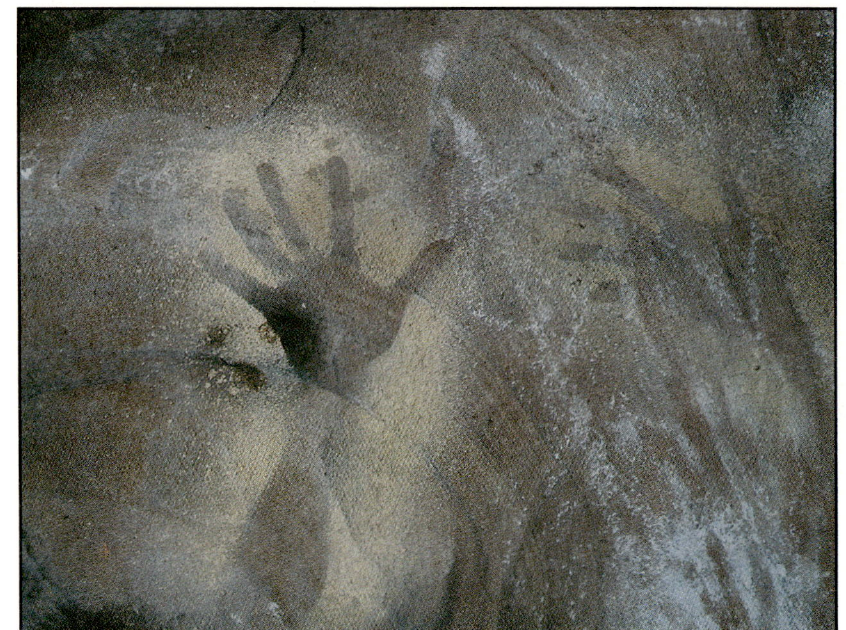

Plate 29.
Monitoring of pigment loss by specialised photography: A hand-stencil site near Gosford, New South Wales, where photographic monitoring is being undertaken. The enlargement shown in Plate 30 is taken from the thumb and forefinger area of the stencil on the right hand side of the photograph. Photograph by Pam Bagatella.

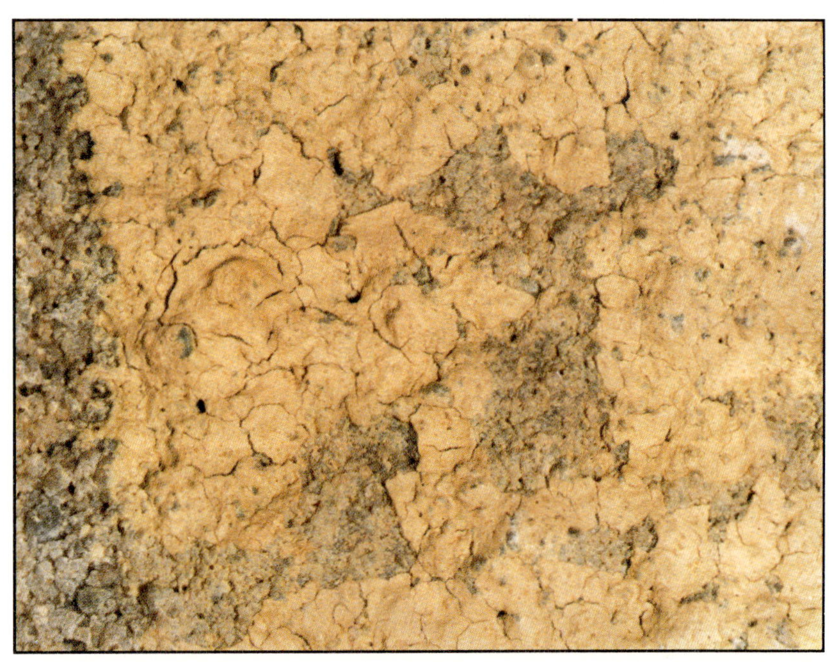

Plate 30.
Monitoring of pigment loss by specialised photography: Enlargement of pigment surface taken from rightmost stencil of previous Plate. The loss of pigment results from cracking and flaking in discrete lumps such that repeated photography will monitor the rate of pigment loss. Photograph by Pam Bagatella.

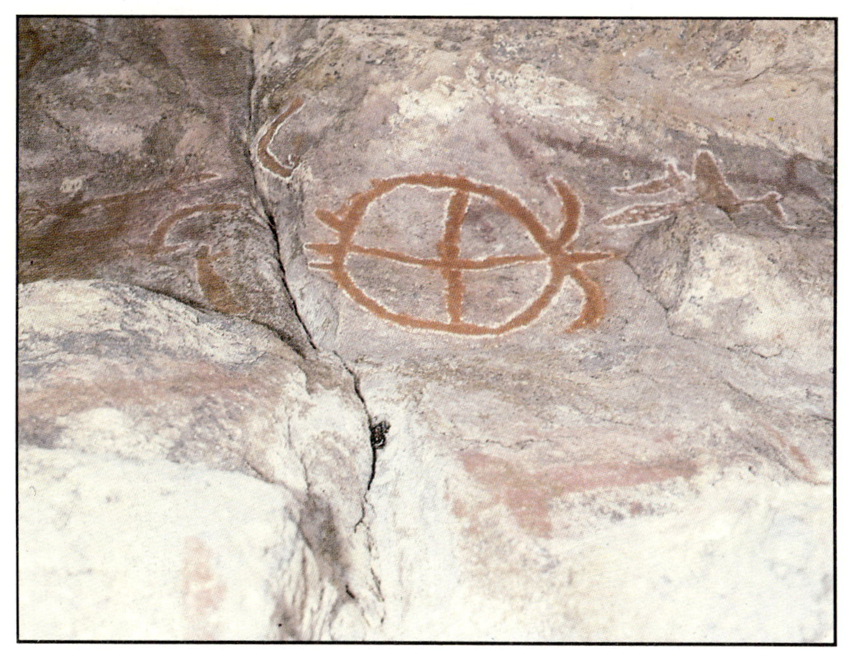

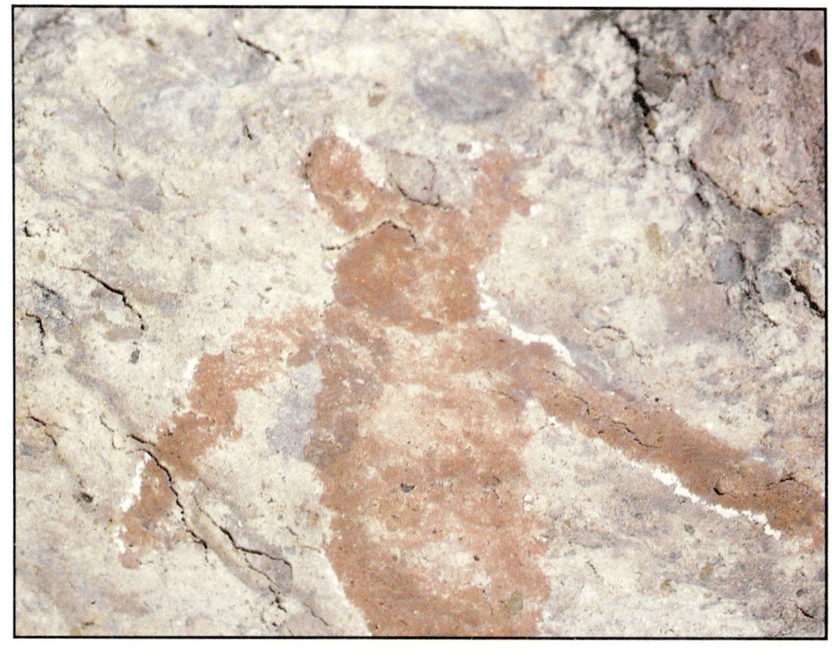

Plates 31 *(above) and* **32** *(below). Monitoring of white pigment loss: A site at Flinders Island, North Queensland containing red ochre figures with white outline in various stages of deterioration. It is appropriate to monitor photographically white pigment loss prior to any use of consolidants.*

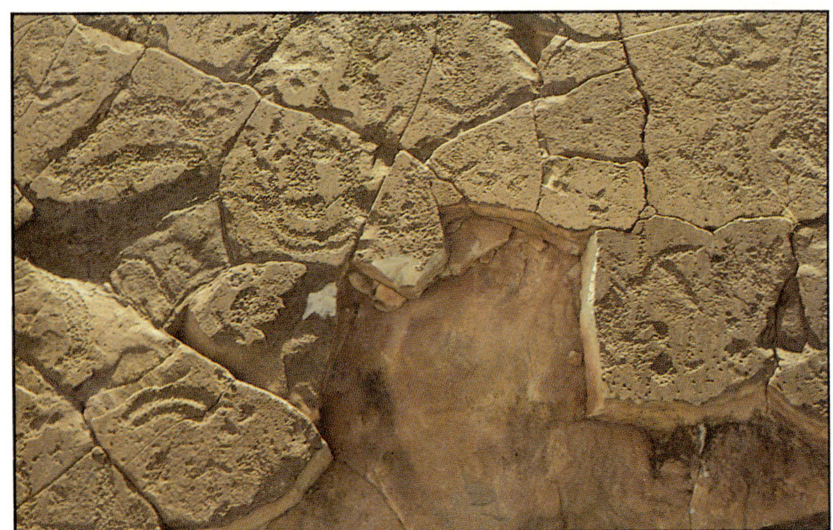

Plate 33.
Conservation of engravings: Engraved cap rock which has been removed from a site at Mootwingee, New South Wales. Note that adjoining cap rock still in place has become loose and partly dislodged.

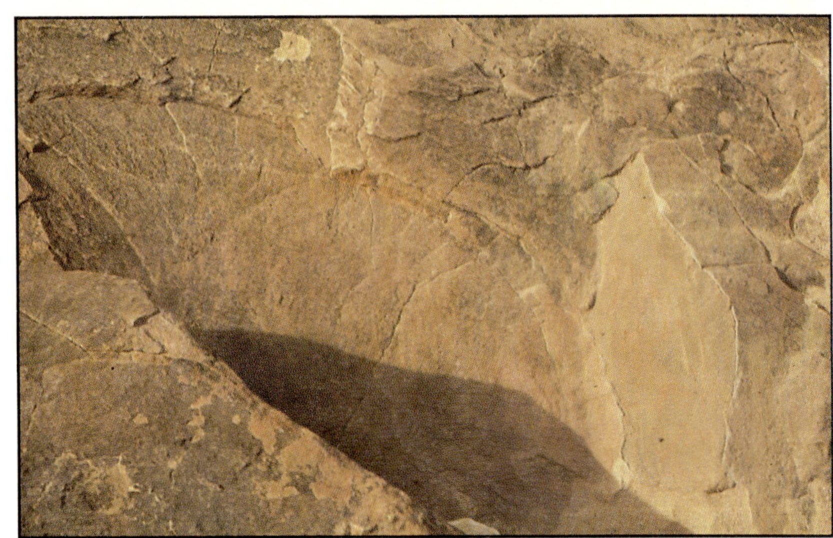

Plate 34.
Conservation of engravings: A trial area where missing cap rock has been filled with a coloured sand and lime mortar mix. Note that an exact colour match is almost impossible to obtain.

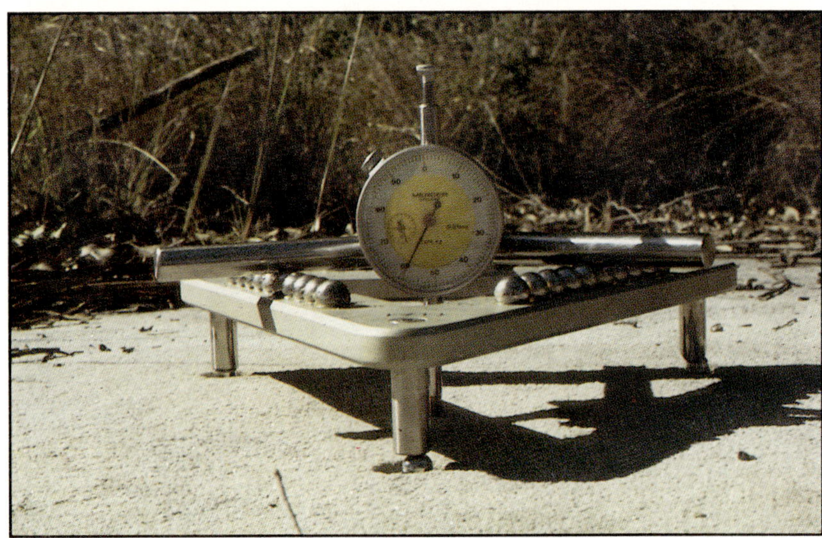

Plate 35.
The traversing micro-erosion meter (TMEM): The TMEM used to monitor surface rock erosion. The meter uses an engineers' dial gauge mounted on a metal frame which sits on three reference studs permanently emplaced in the rock.